# LEADERSHIP
# DEFENSE

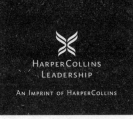

HarperCollins
LEADERSHIP

An Imprint of HarperCollins

# LEADERSHIP
# DEFENSE

## MASTERING PROGRESSIVE DISCIPLINE
## AND STRUCTURING TERMINATIONS

# PAUL FALCONE

Published by HarperCollins Leadership, an imprint of HarperCollins Focus LLC.

Published in association with Kevin Anderson & Associates: https://www.ka-writing.com/.

**Topic 5:** From "Beyond Harassment 101: Opening Culture-Change Discussions with Your Team." *SHRM HR Daily Newsletter*, July 30, 2019. Copyright 2019 by the Society for Human Resource Management. **Topic 7:** From "Team Angst and Brokering Peace in the COVID-19 Era." *SHRM HR Daily Newsletter*, July 7, 2020. Copyright 2020 by the Society for Human Resource Management. **Topic 8:** From "Rumor Mongers and Gossipers: How to Stop 'Stirring the Pot.'" *SHRM HR Daily Newsletter*, October 13, 2019. Copyright 2021 by the Society for Human Resource Management. **Topic 14:** From "When Documenting, Beware: Missteps Can Sink Your Ship in Court." *SHRM HR Daily Newsletter*, August 29, 2016. Copyright 2016 by the Society for Human Resource Management. **Topic 21:** From "Vetting the Record Before Recommending Termination." *SHRM HR Daily Newsletter*, March 2, 2021. Copyright 2021 by the Society for Human Resource Management. **Topic 25:** From "Handling Employees Who Quit—Then Change Their Minds." *SHRM HR Daily Newsletter*, December 13, 2019. Copyright 2019 by the Society for Human Resource Management. **Topic 26:** From "If I Can't Fire Someone, Can I Lay Him Off Instead?" *SHRM HR Daily Newsletter*, March 4, 2020. Copyright 2020 by the Society for Human Resource Management. All of the above used by permission of the publisher. All rights reserved.

Any internet addresses, phone numbers, or company or product information printed in this book are offered as a resource and are not intended in any way to be or to imply an endorsement by HarperCollins Leadership, nor does HarperCollins Leadership vouch for the existence, content, or services of these sites, phone numbers, companies, or products beyond the life of this book.

This book is written as a source of information only. The information contained in this book should by no means be considered a substitute for the advice, decisions, or judgment of the reader's professional advisors.

All efforts have been made to ensure the accuracy of the information contained in this book as of the date published. The author and the publisher expressly disclaim responsibility for any adverse effects arising from the use or application of the information contained herein.

ISBN 978-1-4002-3013-6 (eBook)
ISBN 978-1-4002-3005-1 (TP)

Library of Congress Control Number: 2021951252

Printed in the United States of America
22 23 24 25 26 LSC 10 9 8 7 6 5 4 3 2 1

# CONTENTS

■ ■ ■

# INTRODUCTION

Leadership defense is a topic that sometimes gets short shrift because more attention is paid to motivating and inspiring employees so they experience satisfaction and engagement in the workplace. That positive outlook is so important, but equally important is disciplining and terminating problematic employees, because it's a rare organization that has only exceptional employees.

As much as we may think we hire the best and brightest, we can't really know what's in their hearts. And although thorough interview rounds, preemployment testing, criminal background checks, and reference checks all play critical roles in making "high-probability hires," there's still no guarantee that all who join your team will have altruistic and selfless motives to help you as their leader and the company overall to grow and thrive.

Of course, not all problematic workers come from external hires. Managers sometimes inherit problematic performers via internal transfers or layoffs in other departments, and sometimes entitlement mentalities and victim syndromes simply develop on their own among legacy employees.

In short, any employee at any given time may be facing severe personal problems or simply dislike working in your group or with certain members of your team. Or a successful worker from another department may resent the new challenges your department presents or have difficulty getting over past hurts or current perceived indignities.

However such problems find their way into the workplace, you'll no doubt be required to deal with them at some point in your career. The goal isn't to judge anyone; it's simply to observe the situation and then remedy it professionally and respectfully. But if anyone refuses to reinvent themselves and their relationship to you and the rest of your team, then the leadership defense strategies discussed in this book should help you address the situation constructively and directly.

This book focuses on concrete, hard-core, practical leadership land mines that may await even the most well-meaning or otherwise successful managers. Be sure to rely on these guiding principles so you don't get caught in a snare you didn't see coming. This isn't meant to make you paranoid; instead, it's meant to raise your awareness, so you come to rely more fully on your gut, intuition, or sixth sense. You need to make sure you know how to follow these internal pulses when they tell you that something may be going wrong. Equally important, you need to know when, how, and to whom to disclose your concerns so that you build successful alliances within your company and create the proper record when problematic employee performance or conduct may occur in your group. Mastering these best practices in leadership defense strategies will help protect both you and your company.

## DISCLAIMER

Note: Throughout this book, I interchange the use of *his* and *her*, and I provide examples of fictitious men and women. Obviously, all situations described in these pages can apply to anyone. Further, please bear in mind at all times that this book is not intended as a legal guide to the complex issues surrounding progressive discipline, termination, and other aspects of your employment practices. Because the book does not purport to render legal advice, it should not be used in place of a licensed practicing attorney when proper legal counsel and guidance become necessary. You must rely on your attorney to render a legal opinion that is related to actual fact situations.

# PART 1

# TOUGH CONVERSATIONS, CONSTRUCTIVE CONFRONTATION, AND HOLDING EMPLOYEES ACCOUNTABLE

This section shows how to handle some of the most common and challenging problems that arise in many workplaces: poor attitudes, bullying, swearing, harassment (especially sexual harassment), gossip, rumormongers, snitches, even body odor. I'll describe how to have tough conversations with people about these problems, how to hold employees accountable for their behavior, how to mediate disputes among workers, how to avoid "off-the-record" conversations, and how to confront problems head-on, because avoiding them is *not* the best approach!

■ ■ ■

# ADDRESSING ATTITUDE PROBLEMS

One of the most common challenges facing managers is dealing with employee attitude problems, typically evidenced when employees roll their eyes, sigh, and use antagonistic body language. Trying to stop such "silent" behavior is difficult because employees can so easily deny it.

Frequently, managers tend to avoid confronting employees who "cop a 'tude" because the path of least resistance is avoidance and because the whole matter seems so slippery. After all, as a manager, you don't want to come across as touchy or overly sensitive. Still, feelings of resentment linger and too often result in the employee being publicly shunned and isolated. Sometimes those pent-up emotions result in a public shouting match when some proverbial last straw is broken, and by then the situation is out of control.

There are two key points to keep in mind when attempting to eradicate this all-too-common workplace problem. First, tell the person in private how you *perceive* her actions and how she makes you feel. Be specific and paint a picture with words so that the employee clearly understands the behaviors in question. Ask for her help in solving the perception problem that exists and make a mutual commitment to hear that person's side of the story and better the situation.

Second, avoid the term *attitude* in your discussion and replace it with words like *behavior* or *conduct,* which are much more neutral and objective. The word *attitude* is subjective and inflammatory and typically escalates disagreement by fostering feelings of resentment and anger. More important, courts have interpreted *attitude problems* as being mere differences of opinion or personality conflicts. It is therefore critical that you avoid that specific term in any of your conversations or disciplinary documentation.

When attempting to fix a communication problem that exists with one of your staff members, approach the matter by painting a picture with words like this:

> Lisa, I need your help. You know they say that perception is reality until proven otherwise. I feel like you're either angry with me or angry with the rest of the group. I may be off in my assumption, but that's an honest assessment of what you're giving off. I don't know if anything's bothering you or if you feel that I can be more supportive of you in any way, but please let me know if that's the case.
>
> Otherwise, though, understand that *you make me feel* embarrassed in front of other members of the staff when you roll your eyes upward, sigh, and then say, "Okay, I'll get it done!" Your body language is also confrontational when you cock your head back and place your hands on your hips.
>
> Do you feel it's inappropriate for me to ask you to complete your work on time? Should I even have to follow up with you regarding project completion deadlines, or should it be your responsibility to keep me abreast of the status of your projects? *How would you feel* if you were the manager and one of your staff members responded that way to you in front of others? Likewise, *how*

*would it make you feel* if I responded to your questions with that tone in my voice or that body language? Wouldn't you feel that I was disrespectful or condescending toward you, especially if I did it in front of the rest of the group?

Notice the highlights in the paragraph above: "You make me feel . . ." and "How would you feel . . ." are common phrases that invoke feelings of awareness in others. Feelings aren't right or wrong—they just are. When combining such phrases with an opening statement like "There's a difference in perception here," employees are usually much more willing to hear your side of the story objectively. After all, there are two sides to every story, and employees typically won't deny that they're partially responsible for the problem if it's presented in the right way. What they often want, however, is to be heard and to gain your attention as their manager. Therefore, seize this opportunity to fix the problem verbally by declaring a truce and listening with an objective ear.

# 2

## DEALING WITH EXCESSIVE SWEARING

### PUTTING A QUICK END TO BAD HABITS

As the saying goes, it's sometimes not *what* you say but *how* you say it (and whom you say it to). For example, if an employee stubs his finger in the drawer and shouts, "Oh, f---!" that could be a disciplinary offense that results in a written warning, but it's very unlikely to be cause for termination.

On the other hand, if your subordinate looks at you and shouts, "F--- you!" then it's pretty safe to assume you have a summary dismissal on your hands. Egregious and insubordinate conduct aimed at the supervisor personally allows you little room as an employer to reason, "Well, I'll just give him a warning this time so that he doesn't do that again." If a company were to waive terminating an individual under such circumstances, it could be remiss in its responsibilities for two reasons: First, it would appear irresponsible for allowing such inappropriate conduct to potentially continue and for creating a record of its failure to act. Second, it could create a dangerous precedent for future occurrences of gross insubordination and potentially harassing behavior. After all, if the company didn't terminate under those circumstances, what would justify a termination for someone else in the future?

When an individual takes pride in using language that's more colorful than you'd like, and especially if a coworker puts you on notice that she's not comfortable hearing that type of language in the workplace, respond to the offending employee this way:

Jim, I called this meeting with you in private in my office because we've got a situation that's come up that I'll need your help in solving. Up to now, you've been pretty loose with your language, and I know you tend to use colorful words to make others laugh. And while we all appreciate your sense of humor, we've been put on notice that some folks on the team feel like it's getting out of hand. Whenever we're put on notice as a company that language or behavior potentially offends anyone, we've got to notch things back a bit so that everyone feels comfortable again. I'll need your help in fixing this perception that a problem exists, and I'd like your commitment now that we won't be hearing any expletives or inappropriate sayings from this point forward. Will you support me in that?

That's a very reasonable opener and one that most people will be able to accommodate.

What happens, however, if Jim tells you that he really can't help himself? In fact, he's not even aware of when he's using foul language because it's such an integral part of who he is. His family used that language from the time he was born, his friends used that kind of language when he was growing up, and well, there's really not too much he can do about it. Besides, we're all friends in the group, aren't we? Can't we all agree to just keep things the same? What's all the fuss about anyway? When the justifications and rationalizations come out, it's time to lay down the law a bit more sternly:

Jim, you're not hearing me. This isn't about you any longer—it's about your coworkers and our company. When someone puts us on notice that they're not comfortable with the curses and loose banter and jokes that have arguably become pervasive in the workplace, there's a whole new paradigm in play. At this point, we no longer have the discretion to laugh it off and ignore it. If we do, we can have a hostile work environment claim levied at us, and as you know, hostile work environment claims are a subset of sexual harassment, which fall under our company's antidiscrimination policy.

In short, we're putting you on notice that the language and behavior have to stop immediately. If you really feel you can't accommodate our request, then you may have to make an employment decision. If you honestly can't or won't stop at this point, you'll either have to resign or be terminated for cause should this occur again.

I don't like having this conversation with you because you're an excellent worker and one of our most popular employees, but you've got to understand this and get it right: as much as we enjoy working with you, we can't allow you to expose our company to a hostile work environment claim.

In that case, here's what the record would look like: Employees inform company that they're no longer comfortable with foul language and inappropriate jokes made by Jim Smith. Company does nothing to amend the employee's behavior and allows the foul language to continue. Employees who made the complaint sue the company for failing to take reasonable action to fix the problem. Do you see the challenge we're facing and why I need your help now?

Once you couch the legal concerns in such a straightforward manner, even the most steadfast offenders will take you seriously. If you need any additional fodder to convince Jim of the urgent need to change his behavior, you can include the following:

Oh, and, Jim, there's one more thing: I'm not saying this to frighten you, but I want you to be fully educated. If the company were to be sued, you could also be named as an individual defendant in the lawsuit. In fact, in cases when the company warns the employee and the employee refuses to change his ways, he may be considered to be acting "outside the course and scope of his employment." And under those circumstances, the company's legal team wouldn't necessarily protect you. You'd have to find your own lawyer and pay the damages that arise from the claim.

There are actually two separate legal issues here, Jim: First, there's the concept of personal liability. Second, there's the "out of scope" concept, which speaks to whether the organization will indemnify if the employee is held personally liable. You don't want to go anywhere near either of these two legal issues. We don't pay you enough money to risk your home and your bank account for work-related lawsuits, so any time you find yourself slipping back into your old ways, be sure and stop by my office so that I can remind you about the risks you're assuming when it comes to foul language in the workplace.

If he doesn't take you seriously after that discussion and persists in his argument that this is all silly, put your concerns and expectations in written form, either as a written warning or letter of clarification (which doesn't count as formal disciplinary action because it doesn't contain any consequence language stating that "failure to demonstrate immediate and sustained improvement may result in further action, up to and including dismissal"). Seeing things in writing often escalates the sense of urgency.

# 3

## STOPPING BULLIES IN THEIR TRACKS

Schoolyard bullying—the torment of one child by another—has long been a challenge for students and teachers alike, and it is getting more attention in the workplace as well. Much like their schoolyard counterparts, adult bullies tend to be insecure people who are easily threatened by others. When they sense a nonconfrontational style in peers and subordinates or when they feel threatened, they may turn their insecurity outward and launch attacks aimed at diminishing the self-worth of their intended targets. They may taunt and tease others to increase their own perceived power through humiliation; it's easy to see how this workplace issue may contribute to a toxic work environment.

Any incident in which a worker is abused, threatened, intimidated, teased, or ridiculed can be grouped under the category of intrusive and harassing behaviors, and such emotional and psychological violence should be taken seriously in your organization. The aggression may be verbal, physical (as in blocking someone's way), or visual (as in leering or "staring someone down"). Although prevalent in the workplace, bullying tends to be far less covered by legislation than, for example, sexual harassment or racial discrimination.

And because it can be subtle and easily denied, bullying may be difficult to prove.

Research shows that a bully is just as likely to be a woman as a man. In the workplace, the bullying comes from bosses the majority of the time. When a staff member complains to you that he feels he's being stripped of his dignity or publicly humiliated by his boss, you may have a bullying situation on your hands. Despite the sports folklore of coaches who humiliate and browbeat student athletes to supposedly get the most out of them and to help them "be their best," bullying in the workplace destroys morale for those who witness it and may expose your company to severe financial damages.

Employees often fear going directly to their department head or to HR to complain about an immediate supervisor for fear of retaliation. It becomes all the more important that you proactively address any incidents as soon as they surface, even if no formal complaints are made by the bullied staff member:

> Sarah, I called this meeting with you this afternoon because I witnessed the staff meeting that you held with your team this morning and was concerned about how you apparently handled it. I saw you engage in something I would call a public humiliation session with Ron, and from what I could see, your attacks were intended to strip him of his dignity in front of the rest of the group. Can you picture the meeting and specifically what I'm talking about? [*Pause.*]

At this point, the manager may launch into an all-out defense to justify her actions: "Ron did the stupidest thing I've ever seen. He called a client on the phone and said . . ."

> Sarah, this isn't about the merits of your argument, and I certainly don't need a justification of any sort for your behavior. Whatever

Ron did or didn't do is not what we're here about. We're here about your response and the behavior that you demonstrated in that staff meeting in front of the rest of the team earlier today.

Let me be clear. Bullying your subordinates for any reason and under any circumstance violates company policy. More significantly, it makes me lose faith in your ability to lead and your ultimate suitability for the position you're in.

If I had to describe your behavior today, I would say that you humiliated, overruled, ignored, and isolated your subordinate in front of his peers. That's bad for morale, bad for teamwork, and creates a culture based on fear. As a company, we pay for that over time in lost efficiency, turnover, absenteeism, and unnecessary separation packages and lawsuits. Your actions this morning created a tremendous liability for our company, both in terms of stress-related health and safety exposure as well as the costs associated with unnecessary turnover. Stripping people of their dignity or humiliating them publicly is no longer an option for you. I'm here to make sure that you don't do that again. Do you understand my reasoning? [*Yes.*]

Good. I'm choosing not to put this in the form of a written warning at this point, Sarah. Just know that if I ever again have to address this with you, my recommendation to human resources will be that they pursue the matter as aggressively as possible, including a consideration of immediate discharge.

Okay, you threw the book at her, yet by not documenting your meeting in the form of a written warning, you let her off fairly easily. That's certainly your right. Just be sure and keep a close eye on Sarah and her staff to make sure that no further flare-ups arise. In addition, jot down the highlights of this conversation as well as the date, place, and time so you can refer back to it should you ever need to. And don't forget to give HR a heads-up just so they're aware of the problem.

If you feel strongly that another such incident should result in immediate termination, you're best off documenting your findings now in a final written warning rather than a simple discussion. Don't miss an opportunity to document egregious misconduct. It may be harder to terminate after the next offense if you neglected to document this infraction and establish a record of ongoing and repeated violations of company policy.

# 4

# ADDRESSING SEXUAL HARASSMENT

Sexual harassment concerns employers of all sizes and in all industries. Recent headlines alleging sexual misconduct, abusive behaviors, and even assault have led to the fall of entertainment moguls, on-air talent, and politicians in the highest offices of the land.

The underlying problem stems not from a lack of knowledge, however; instead, corporate cultures sometimes inadvertently allow toxic behaviors to pepper the workplace. In other cases, the behavior of individual managers toward subordinates or peers perpetuates ongoing problems, creating both corporate and individual liability that becomes difficult to defend in he-said, she-said situations.

Worse, many executives, managers, and supervisors don't know that individual liability can be imputed to them for certain claims, such as harassment, aiding and abetting discrimination, and/or retaliation (depending on the state in which they work). While managers are not liable under every employment law, there are several federal and state laws that may impart individual liability. Harassment or bullying based on a protected characteristic, including sexual harassment, often triggers such claims, and it's only when leaders find themselves on the sharp end of the investigative spear that they realize they may have risked personal assets like their homes and bank accounts for engaging in egregious misconduct that can somehow be linked to another person's sex, gender, or sexual orientation.

Although it's easier to simply add more training to this problem, the key solution is to tie employees' behaviors to personal liability. For example, let's look at a young male television producer working in California who has a top-rated show and feels justified in hitting on all the young female production assistants and interns. How can you turn around an aggressive personality and cocky arrogance when the individual feels he can't be touched? Very simply: hit him in the pocketbook. Watch how it works:

[General Manager]: Ted, as the general manager of the studio, I invited Paul from human resources to join us for a discussion that may be difficult for you to hear but that's critically important to you at this stage of your professional development and career. I know you've got a hit show, and you're a hot commodity in town, but we've learned about something that could seriously hold you back or damage your reputation and the reputation of the show if you don't gain control of it quickly. Paul, can I ask you to provide Ted with more details?

[HR]: Sure. Ted, what I've heard is that you may be hitting on several of the younger female production assistants and interns. I haven't witnessed this, but I've heard through some people on set that this may be happening and making people feel uncomfortable. That's why we're here today. First, we need to remind you of the show's antiharassment policy and our duty to investigate these allegations. If you're engaging in this behavior, you risk violating our policy, which could lead to adverse action against you.

Second, most executives in your line of work and at your level of success lose sight of some of the basics—namely, that not only can you lose your job for engaging in violations of the show's anti-harassment policy, but as a high-net-worth individual, you're a high-profile target with deep pockets and any lawyer in town would love to get their hands on some type of sexual harassment claim coming out of here because there are two juicy targets—the studio and the production executive. Plaintiffs' lawyers know that we need to avoid negative publicity at all costs and will likely settle any claim as quickly as possible. That works to their favor and means we're a juicy target for a lawsuit, and so are you individually.

So, I want to be clear about this and make sure you're aware that your behavior is risking your job and potentially your personal assets. We don't pay you enough to risk your home, your savings account, your car, and whatever else for unwittingly creating a perception that you're hitting on multiple young women on your team. Bear in mind as well that, in many states, you can be sued personally for up to $50,000 of your own money for inappropriate managerial conduct; in California, however, there's no limit. I'd be doing you a disservice if I didn't inform you of this, and I'd never want you to learn about potential personal liability for this type of behavior only after being served with a sexual harassment lawsuit.

Further, remember that under the code of conduct, you're not allowed to date anyone on your team who is a subordinate. As the executive producer, you're the top of the totem pole, so that means everyone on your team is a subordinate. Accordingly, we do not condone managers engaging in romantic relationships with subordinates. At a minimum, if you sense that a romantic relationship is beginning, you have an affirmative obligation to disclose it to us immediately, and we'll decide how to handle the reporting relationship so that the show is protected from potential claims.

Your success is our success, Ted, and we certainly want it to continue, but we can't allow you to damage the show by your unprofessional behavior. Do you have any questions about what I've shared with you just now? [*No—I wasn't aware of any of this.*] Okay, good then. I hope you have a much clearer understanding of how quickly things can go wrong. As mentioned, we will need to investigate this matter further, so we will be in touch. My door's always open if I can help with anything, and please know that I'll always be here for you, if and when you need advice or guidance.

Nothing makes more sense to successful executives, salespeople, and yes—even Hollywood directors—than the potential of them being fired for sexual harassment and, further, getting hit in their pocketbook via an individual lawsuit. Hopefully, he got the message and will think very carefully about his behavior going forward.

# CULTURE SHIFT

## CREATING A HEALTHY AND RESPECTFUL WORK ENVIRONMENT

**B**ecause sexual harassment remains a problem in many work-places (despite years of mandatory training for supervisors to prevent it), getting in front of the problem requires raising accountability and an awareness of inclusion and respect in the office or on the shop floor. That, however, requires full-scale culture change, which is not something that can be taught in one or two hours via videos, rules, and definitions.

Training like that may be a good start for ensuring a minimum understanding of a company's policies, reporting requirements, and caveats surrounding retaliation, but it likely won't effectuate real cultural change; that can come only when frontline managers companywide assume full responsibility for ensuring a friendly and inclusive work environment by modeling the appropriate behaviors themselves. Launching such a program starts by discussing the effects of inappropriate conduct and how one change in everyone's approach can make a better working experience for all.

Absolute success is likely impossible, but managers' words, actions, and conduct will influence employees more than they imagine. How can you, as a corporate leader, ensure that harassment doesn't plague your workplace? The answer lies in transparent communication and expectations that are set appropriately. Building a harassment-free workplace is all about heart: respect, inclusion, selfless leadership, and the sense that colleagues have one another's backs should the need arise. The proactive group solution builds coworkers' emotional intelligence. While raising people's awareness of how they come across to others is sometimes challenging, it's a valuable exercise that proffers real-life lessons that will likely stand the test of time.

Here's how your opening statement to your department or team might sound:

Folks, I called this meeting to discuss a topic that's of concern to all of us: sexual harassment. Now, don't roll your eyes. I'm serious about this. Nothing defines us more as a team than the way we treat and respect one another. I'm holding this meeting not because I have to, but because I want to. The scope and tone of our interpersonal relationships is key to our getting along. I want you to know that I always have your backs, but certain behaviors and forms of conduct cross the line, and the consequences can be swift and severe.

First, sexual harassment falls under our company's antidiscrimination policy. Further, our code of conduct sets the standard for how we're expected to treat one another in terms of both the letter and the spirit of the law. There are real consequences for people accused and found guilty of violating this particular policy, including disciplinary action or even outright termination for an egregious first offense. In other words, the policy has teeth, and the company is willing to enforce it and won't turn a blind eye.

Next, keeping this defense strategy in mind, it's even more important that we discuss our offense strategy. What do I and what should you expect a healthy workplace to look like? We need to make sure we have a high enough level of trust in and respect for one another that we can assume good intentions when faced with challenges. I expect you all to practice selfless leadership in putting others' needs ahead of your own. I want our group to be the team that pays it forward, supports one another, and fosters a sense of appreciation and gratitude for working here. I want us to be a team that others look up to and emulate, not just for our productivity but because of our camaraderie. I want ours to be a team that others want to join because we're there for one another and because we focus on each other's best interests.

Finally, when in doubt, err on the side of compassion—we're all trying our best. That's the team I'd like to see us become, and that's the model you might want to consider when you manage teams of your own throughout your career.

Make this topic an occasional touchpoint at weekly meetings and a formal matter at quarterly check-ins. You set the role-model behavior for others to follow and demonstrate how this works by your actions. Be willing to apologize first when there's any doubt about intentions or actions, praise in public and censure in private, make light of misunderstandings, and inject a sense of humor in the day-to-day. That's the team your staffers will want to work with and for. That's the behavior that will be honored and rewarded across your department.

# THE DANGER OF
# OFF-THE-RECORD CONVERSATIONS

Too many leaders have inadvertently stepped on land mines because they either said too much or otherwise made promises or guarantees that they simply couldn't keep. One common area where such land mines exist has to do with overpromising confidentiality. If an employee asks to speak with you off the record, train yourself right now to respond like this:

> *Maybe.* It all depends on what you have to say. If it has to do with one of three things, Laura, then I can't promise confidentiality because I'll have an affirmative obligation to disclose it to senior leadership. The three things are harassment or discrimination, potential violence in the workplace, or an inherent conflict of interest with the company's business practices. If it doesn't have to do with any of those three things, I'd be happy to speak with you. But if it does, then understand that you may not want to tell me because I'll be obligated to bring the matter to the attention of senior management or HR.

Wait! Is it reasonable for leaders to instruct their subordinates *not* to tell them something that's on their minds or that's otherwise bothering them? I would argue yes. If employees want to talk off the record and not have the information escalate, then they shouldn't tell their bosses if one of the three categorical areas above is in question. Likewise, leaders need to know not to provide blanket authorization to talk about anything and everything on the employee's mind because they may have to disclose the matter, breaching their agreement of confidentiality with the employee and that individual's trust.

Here are some common examples in which you shouldn't promise absolute confidentiality when an employee asks to speak off the record:

- "I'm afraid that Ashley is feeling threatened and harassed by Matthew's constant requests for a date. She told me not to say anything to anyone, but I don't know what to do and want to help her."
- "Cole, an IT programmer, pulled a bullet out of his shirt pocket and banged it on his desk three times this morning, shouting: 'No one better bother me today.' I think we all got pretty freaked out because we know he keeps rifles in the trunk of his car so that he could visit the rifle range after work every night. Wasn't that weird?"
- "I know you're not my supervisor, but I always enjoy spending time with you. I have an opportunity to moonlight with XYZ Corporation. I know they're a direct competitor of ours, but they're willing to pay me $60 an hour for twenty hours of work every week over the next three months to help them meet a project deadline. It sure would be helpful to make that extra money, but I wouldn't want anyone else to know. I'm really excited!"

In situations like these, you have an affirmative obligation to disclose your findings. Why? Because in the eyes of the law, once an employee places a company leader (that is, a supervisor, manager, director, VP, and the like) on notice, then the *entire company* is deemed to have been placed on notice.

Here's how it works in reality: An ex-employee of your company decides to meet with an attorney to discuss what she believes was a wrongful termination from the company. During questioning, the employee volunteers to her attorney that she felt threatened by her supervisor on occasion because of his aggressiveness and disparaging comments about her weight. The lawyer questions further and learns that other indirect comments were made about her age and her choice of clothing (along with occasional references about her "sexy legs" and, on one occasion, large breasts).

Bingo! The attorney now believes the ex-employee has claims against the employer for wrongful termination, discrimination, and harassment, based on age, sex, and, arguably, disability (due to the supervisor's weight comment)—potentially entailing the awarding of punitive damages. The next question is key. The lawyer asks, "Did you ever inform anyone in management about how you were feeling?" The employee hesitates and responds, "Well, yes and no. I told Jim, who's a supervisor, but he's not my supervisor. And I made him promise me to keep it confidential, which he did and which I appreciate. Besides, I'd never want him to get caught in the middle of any of this or get into any kind of trouble."

Too late! The case for discrimination and harassment has now swung decidedly in the plaintiff attorney's favor, and Jim, the company's trusted supervisor, is going to be the main reason why. He'll be taken through a series of interrogatories and depositions and may ultimately be asked to take the stand to establish why he, as a leader of the company, failed to affirmatively disclose the harassment and discrimination complaint that was made to him. His sheepish and apologetic response will sound something along the lines of, "Well, Gabrielle asked me to keep it confidential, and I wanted to respect her request."

Boom! The land mine just exploded. The entire crux of the case will be shifted to Jim's failure to disclose the harassment he learned of. The plaintiff's lawyer will skillfully argue that, in the eyes of the law, once Jim was placed on notice as a supervisor or manager, the entire company was deemed to have been placed on notice, and the company did absolutely nothing to stop the egregious misconduct that subjected Gabrielle to harassing and discriminatory behavior. So much for being a nice guy! Jim, as a supervisor, fell for the biggest sucker punch in the book: he failed to disclose something that he had an obligation to escalate to senior management or HR. He'll unfortunately feel the full brunt of his decision because the entire lawsuit will rest on his ultimate failure to do his job.

Plaintiffs' lawyers aren't in the business of protecting old friendships. Their job is to expose a company's shortcomings, and "company," in this instance, refers to the individual leaders who didn't have a clear understanding of their responsibilities under the law. Therefore, it's critical that you avoid overpromising confidentiality. This particular error or oversight on leaders' parts has gotten them into tremendous amounts of trouble and has cost people their jobs.

Remember, if anyone asks you to speak off the record, respond "Maybe," not "Yes"! Then follow the script above to clarify your expectations before the employee lets loose with her innermost secrets. Employees may not know how much trouble they're getting you into, but now you know how to protect yourself from this particular land mine.

# 7

# MEDIATING EMPLOYEE DISPUTES AND THE ART OF CONSTRUCTIVE CONFRONTATION

Every line manager in corporate America has felt frustrated over employee tensions and unresolved conflict. And let's face it: there's typically more than enough work that needs to be done without involving hurt feelings, resentment, and that walking-on-eggshells sensation that makes you feel more like a referee than a manager.

With the critical need for retention of key talent, managers have to find ways to get their people "plugged in" again or else face premature turnover. However, your staff members will almost always take the path of least resistance with one another—which is avoidance—rather than address problem issues head-on. As the manager, you must intervene in a mediating role to ensure that a lack of communication doesn't lead to performance problems or turnover.

Pretending that a problem doesn't exist or allowing staff members to work out problems on their own may be a safe strategy when a new interpersonal conflict first arises; however, once that initial frustration has festered, it becomes time to step in. When two of your staff members are at war, meet with each individual separately and explain how you intend to resolve the problem:

Sam, I'm meeting with you one-on-one and will do the same with Christina once you and I are done. I want you to understand how together we're going to resolve the underlying tension that's become fairly obvious between the two of you.

First, I want to hear your side of the story in this meeting, then I'll share that with Christina when I meet with her later today. I'll then want to hear Christina's side of the story, and I'll share her feedback with you before the three of us come together as a group. This way, everyone will know everyone else's issues, and we can come together and focus on *how* to resolve it.

In short, we'll solve this in three meetings. Our meeting right now, Sam, is the first one. My meeting with Christina right after we're done will be the second one. I'll follow up with you after that and give you her feedback. Finally, we'll have a third meeting tomorrow morning where we can talk this out together. Again, everyone will know the issues, so there won't be any surprises, and we'll solve this like adults, maintaining one another's respect and dignity. Are you clear on how I'm planning on handling this?

At this point, listen to Sam's side of the story. Ask him why Christina may be feeling the way she does, what he'd like to see happen ideally in terms of his relationship with Christina, and what he'd be willing to change about his own behavior to elicit a different response from her in the future.

Afterward, hold the same meeting with Christina, learn her side of the story, and then share her perceptions with Sam afterward. Overall, both need to hear the other person's side of the story in advance from you so they can give it ample consideration and determine how they plan to handle the group meeting that you're about to hold. Assuming that most adults need time to process matters like this and benefit from sleeping on it, hold the meeting first thing the next morning. Set the ground rules of the group meeting with both employees in your office as follows:

Okay, Sam and Christina, I've got two key ground rules that we all have to follow before we begin.

First, you already both know the other person's side of the story, so there should be very few surprises in our meeting this morning. Therefore, you shouldn't hold anything back. This is your chance to get it all out in the open, and if you withhold anything, then you'll have missed a golden opportunity to share your side of the story. This is a once-in-a-career benefit, and I'm not planning on readdressing these pent-up issues and frustrations in the future. We're fixing this now. After our meeting today, I'm rewelcoming you both to the company as if it were your first day of employment. I'm also holding you both accountable for reinventing your working relationship from this point forward. Does that sound like a reasonable approach on my part? [*Yes.*]

Second, everything that you share has to be said with the other person's best interests in mind and in a spirit of constructive feedback. There is no need for attacking and no need for defending in this meeting; this is really more a sensitivity session in which you both get to walk a mile in the other's shoes and hear firsthand how the other is feeling. Do I have your agreement on both of these ground rules? [*Yes.*]

Setting up a meeting with these qualifiers automatically de-escalates feelings of angst or anger in the participants. It also gives you the chance to take a gentle approach to interpersonal issues that, like scars, sometimes run long and deep.

During the group meeting, you'll sometimes notice that each employee will first address concerns directly to you—the mediator.

It will be as if the other person weren't even there. Third-person "he-she" discussions need to be changed into an "I-you" dialogue. To accomplish this shift in audience, simply stop the conversation as soon as one of the participants begins speaking about the other in the third person. Ask the individual to speak directly to the other person as if *you* weren't there. That may appear a little challenging for the participants at first, especially if emotions are running high, but direct communication works best. After all, you're helping them fix *their* problems.

In addition, encourage your two staff members to use the phrases "this is how I feel" and "can you understand why I would feel that way?" Feelings aren't right or wrong—they just are. Since perception is reality until proven otherwise, it's each individual's responsibility to sensitize the other regarding the existence of perceptions that have developed over time.

Knowing that a heightened sense of awareness will allow for the assumption of partial responsibility for an imperfect situation, that element of accountability will serve as the seed of goodwill that helps heal old wounds. For example, if Christina feels bad about her relationship with Sam, shares with him why she feels the way she does, and admits that it takes two to tango and that she's part of the problem, then Sam will likely respond positively to the olive branch that Christina's extending.

Once you've pierced the heart of the combatants, so to speak, then the battle is won. You'll know you're there when they're talking to each other, agreeing that they've got a problem on their hands, and demonstrating a willingness to fix it. These kinds of management interventions aren't normally fact-finding investigations. Instead, they're sensitivity-training sessions where goodwill and openness naturally heal the wounds associated with ego and principle.

Conclude the meeting this way:

Christina and Sam, you've both heard the other person's side of the story now. I'm not asking you to become best friends, but I'm insisting that you both demonstrate respect and open communication toward each other at work from this point forward so that nothing falls through the cracks and becomes a workplace performance problem. Further, as a takeaway, I want both of you to think about what you're willing to change in your own behaviors to elicit a different response from the other person going forward.

I'll end this meeting with two questions. First, do I have your commitment that you'll view the other with goodwill and assume good intentions from this point forward? Second, do you both understand that if the situation doesn't improve and the workflow is negatively affected in any way, my response next time may result in formal progressive discipline rather than a goodwill sit-down like this?

And voilà—you'll have given both employees the opportunity to vent and share their perceptions of the problem. You'll end the meeting on a constructive note with both agreeing to change their behavior. And you'll also create a healthy sense of paranoia in which both realize that if the problem surfaces again, there may be a more formal management response—most likely in the form of a written warning. Congratulations! You've treated your warring parties as adults and held them accountable for fixing the perception problem on their hands.

Remember, no matter how much you care, you can't manage *their* differences. Only they can do that. Still, you can provide a forum for resolving employee disputes that brings out the best in people. Establishing a culture of openness means confronting problems in an environment that's safe and that maintains the individual's dignity. It enhances your position as a leader and establishes your reputation as a fair arbiter of disagreements. There's no better formula for employee retention than treating people with respect, dignity, and a caring ear.

# 8

# DEALING WITH GOSSIPS, RUMORMONGERS, AND SNITCHES

People who gossip about their coworkers' or bosses' personal problems, work styles, or private challenges stir up drama for no good reason. Another problem behavior occurs when employees initiate or perpetuate rumors, even if they lack any foundation of truth or could potentially damage others' reputations or hurt their feelings. And most people know intuitively that playing the tattletale role—that is, snitching—is just plain wrong.

These behaviors occur all the time to differing degrees, but few things in the workplace do more to undermine employee morale and trust than corporate "grapevining" that is allowed to go unaddressed and unchecked. It acts like a worm in an apple, slowly coring away the goodwill and respect that creates camaraderie and trust.

Here's one way to handle these problems. Asking the employee who was the brunt of rumor (we'll call him Corey) whom he suspects originated the rumor isn't really at issue; unless someone voluntarily admits it, blaming or finger-pointing isn't really the end goal of an exercise like this. What is important is how you address the situation and reset expectations with your staff:

Everyone, I've asked Corey to join me in this meeting because a rumor has developed about his personal life. We don't know who originated the rumor, and if any one of you would like to speak with me in private after this meeting about your involvement in starting or perpetuating the rumor, I'd be happy to hear what you have to say.

For now, I want you all to know how hurtful this is. We're a team, and anyone who could raise issues like this against one member of the team raises them against us all. I personally would be very offended and hurt if anyone started or continued a rumor about my personal life, which had nothing to do with my performance at work.

Whether there's any truth to this rumor is not the issue; it's simply none of our business. This is about respect—for each other as individuals and for our team.

Let me be clear: I expect that no one will engage in this type of character assassination or public shaming ever again. I also expect that everyone in our department will stop others from spreading rumors of a personal nature. In short, if you have nothing good to say, say nothing at all. Do I have your agreement and commitment on that on a go-forward basis? [*Yes.*]

Corey, on behalf of the entire team, I'm very sorry for anything that was said that might have hurt or offended you. We'll commit to stopping these types of behaviors in their tracks in the future. Again, my apologies to you on behalf of our team for the inappropriate lapse in judgment that was demonstrated here. Is there anything you'd care to share with the rest of us that I might have missed or that you think is important that we're aware of? [*No.*] Okay, then. Thank you all for coming.

The best course of action is always to address the rumor openly with the group in front of the intended victim and to apologize for the perception problem that was created by someone's lack of discretion.

Now, what if you catch a gossipmonger in the act? Such instances require a firm and immediate response:

> Justin, as a result of your actions, Jasmine has become the brunt of some mean-spirited office banter. As you can imagine, she was embarrassed and humiliated for something she had absolutely nothing to do with. And that leaves me feeling fairly disappointed at your lack of discretion and insensitivity.
>
> Let me be clear. At this point, you have a perception problem on your hands—the perception that you've gossiped and fed the corporate grapevine, which has made our work environment more toxic. I'm holding you fully responsible for your own perception management from this point forward.
>
> I think an apology may be in order here, but I'll leave that up to you. For now, I really want you to think about your actions and how you may have inadvertently made someone look bad in the eyes of her peers, feel diminished, and feel like less of a person. That's very sad, Justin, and I want you to know that I'm counting this as a verbal warning. I want your commitment right now that we'll never have to have a discussion like this again and that, should it occur again, further discipline, up to and including immediate termination, could result. Are we in agreement here? [*Yes—sorry.*]

Mean-spirited actions like this deserve a firm response on the company's part. Also, note the use of guilt (rather than anger) in your approach: "I really want you to think about your actions and how you may have inadvertently made someone look bad in the eyes of her peers, feel diminished, and feel like less of a person." Guilt, in its healthiest sense, can be a most effective human emotion because it helps people look within for partial responsibility to a problem. That should get him thinking about the error of his ways and assuming responsibility for his inappropriate actions.

Finally, snitches need to be addressed as yet another subcategory of this universally human problem. Snitches often hit you with a "Psst. It may be none of my business, so please stop me if you feel I'm being inappropriate by sharing this with you, *but . . .*" And once they've opened up with that disclaimer, they unload all sorts of details on you that typically serve to get their coworkers in trouble. When faced with a snitch who believes she's "doing you the favor" of acting as your eyes and ears, stop her dead in her tracks:

> Rachel, I understand that you believe that I need to know these things, especially since they occur when I'm not in the office or behind closed doors. And I appreciate your always trying to keep me in the loop as to what's going on. But there's a bigger issue that I want to sensitize you to, and it's a moral issue that has a lot to do with principle and doing the right thing.
>
> Not to sound ungrateful or unappreciative, but I don't know that sharing that kind of information about Tiana with me is the right thing for you to do. Don't get me wrong: if you witnessed someone stealing or being harassed, I would want to know about that immediately. But those are serious *misconduct* infractions that could have dire consequences to the company. When it comes to *performance* issues that you become aware of, though, I don't think that you should necessarily feel compelled to volunteer that information.
>
> First of all, I'll probably be able to find that out on my own before too long. Second, it places you into the role of mole or corporate snitch, and when that gets out (which it will sooner or later), you won't be trusted by your peers. And that will bring more

long-term damage to the department than the current performance-related problem that you felt compelled to report. Do you see why sometimes withholding that kind of information may be better for both you and for the department in the long run?

All of these issues—gossiping, rumormongering, and snitching—are sometimes on a slippery slope. And, admittedly, these actions are often taken with little thought of the damage that could be done. Nevertheless, left unaddressed, they can damage team spirit and goodwill. Be direct, be open, and shy away from nothing when it comes to eradicating these insidious forces from the workplace. Your team will benefit, your subordinates will respect and appreciate you, and wrongdoers will learn the errors of their ways before those same types of mistakes wreak havoc on their careers.

# 9

# ADDRESSING BODY ODOR PROBLEMS

**B**ody odor is an especially uncomfortable issue to address because of the personal nature of the problem, and many people are not even aware it's an issue. If they were, there probably wouldn't be a problem! However, some people define taking a bath as jumping into a chlorinated pool, while other folks simply fail to apply deodorant consistently or wear their clothes too many times before washing them. Whatever the case, an odiferous offender shouldn't upset everyone else in the department, and there are tactful ways of handling the matter professionally.

You're best off opening your private conversation by assuming that the individual isn't aware there is a problem. This way, even if he does know, he could pretend that he's being made aware of this problem for the first time and take appropriate measures to correct the situation. Here's a sample conversation launcher:

Andrew, I wanted to meet with you one-on-one in my office because I need to share something with you privately, discreetly, and with as much sensitivity as possible. You may not realize it, but it appears that you may have a body odor problem, and it isn't merely a personal matter—it's a workplace disruption issue that I need your help to repair.

I've had conversations like this with employees before, and usually they're not even aware that the problem exists. I don't mean to make you uncomfortable, but don't mind my asking: Are you aware of the issue, and if so, is this something you can take care of on your own?

Again, this is a fairly comfortable approach that avoids putting anyone on the spot. Assuming the individual is unaware of the issue to begin with, your putting him on notice should be all that's necessary to solve that challenge. You might offer Andrew the option to return home with pay, freshen up, and then return to the office when he's ready. That's a fair and objective way of handling an uncomfortable workplace situation without drama or histrionics.

People with poor hygiene habits may be oblivious to how that can affect others in the workplace. Your conversation links the personal hygiene problem to a workplace performance matter, which places you on clear ground to address the matter as part of the individual's overall performance. You might then choose to end the conversation on a positive note:

Andrew, listen, I'm here to help in any way I can. If you'd like us to set up a fan in your office, or if you'd like to change your schedule so that you could take breaks throughout the day to have time to freshen up, I'd be very supportive of that. Just let me know whatever I could do to help, okay? If you wouldn't mind, though, I'd prefer not to have to address this with you again because it's a bit uncomfortable for me, so is this something you feel you can fix on a go-forward basis?

And that little segue out of your conversation will allow the employee to dash out of your office, run home to shower, and then make sure that he never has to hear those horrible words from anyone else again for the rest of his career!

If the employee begins to offer reasons for his body odor that go beyond mere hygiene (for example, medical issues), stop him before he goes into too much detail. You, as his manager, don't want much information as to the cause of his body odor if it's anything more than failure to use the appropriate amount of soap without looping in human resources.

Instead, let Andrew know that if he needs to seek medical treatment for a health-related condition, he should discuss this with human resources. Human resources will engage in communications with Andrew to determine if he has a disability and will explore in good faith possible accommodations that would allow Andrew to perform the essential functions of his job without undue hardship to the company. This is called the "ADA interactive process."

At a minimum, human resources should encourage Andrew to take time off to go to the doctor as soon as he can get an appointment. And if your company offers an Employee Assistance Program (EAP), human resources should provide him with an EAP brochure so that he can call them and get the appropriate resources he needs to solve the dilemma. If additional accommodations for Andrew's medical condition will be necessary, human resources will advise Andrew that he needs to submit a medical certification (a doctor's note) specifying accommodations that would allow him to effectively perform the essential functions of his job with some form of reasonable accommodation that won't create an undue hardship for the organization.

If, on the other hand, the employee's offensive body odor continues and is not related to a medical condition and remains disruptive to the work environment, you should inform him that coming to work unclean or unkempt disrupts productivity and violates company policy. You can then place him on verbal notice that if you have to address this matter again with him, disciplinary action may follow.

Appropriate disciplinary action in a case like this would most likely be in the form of a documented verbal warning. The nature of this infraction, especially if it has anything to do with obesity, will not lend itself to more progressive forms of discipline like immediate termination or even a final written warning for this first documented offense. Of course, this will depend on your company's progressive discipline practices, but this is probably not a good time to accelerate or skip steps in that process. Generally speaking, start with the first formal step of progressive discipline as outlined in company policy (i.e., a documented verbal warning) and then, if need be, progress to written (second step) and final written (third and final step) warnings.

In contrast, odors may come from a protected medical condition—for example, obesity or colostomy bags. These conditions are not necessarily something your employee can control and will have to be accommodated by you, the employer. In fact, the Americans with Disabilities Act (ADA) and applicable state laws will likely govern these matters, so how you address them may be more than workplace sensitivity: it may be a matter of law. Now that I've gotten your attention, proceed this way:

> Amelia, I need to make you aware of a situation that has come to my attention, and I'll need your help to solve it. A few of your coworkers came to me out of concern for you but also out of concern for themselves. Apparently, there is an odor coming from your desk area that makes it difficult for them to do their work. The odor is

described as being a combination of sweat and urine, and apparently this is the third time they've noticed it. They've asked me to address it with you. I'm here to help resolve the problem, if possible.

If the employee identifies some underlying medical or health issue that could be contributing to the problem, do not continue. Rather, send the employee to human resources. (If your organization does not have an HR department, speak immediately with your boss and in-house attorney, if available.) Under the ADA and applicable state law, you are now likely on notice that the employee may be suffering from a disability, and therefore the company needs to respond to the employee in strict accordance with the ADA. If the employee does not identify some underlying medical or health issue, do not suggest the possibility of one causing the odor. Rather, ask how she could resolve the matter. "I trust that you understand how this could be a problem?" You can also invite her to take advantage of the company's EAP program and discuss any personal issues with human resources if she would prefer.

It's important for you to know that the ADA is a civil rights–oriented antidiscrimination law, which prohibits private employers, among others, from discriminating against qualified individuals with disabilities in applying for a job, hiring, firing, and job training. As such, its intentions are admirable. However, the law has been broadened over the years and provides plaintiffs' attorneys with lots of room to argue its merits and applications to the workplace. In addition, several states have their own versions of the ADA, many of which are even more employee friendly than the federal version. Add the fact that remedies can include punitive damages, and your company could face serious legal exposure.

In addition to defining a disability as a physical or mental impairment (or record of such an impairment) that substantially limits a major life activity, the ADA also covers individuals who are "regarded as" having a disability. Regarded as having a disability is different from an actual disability in that the impairment does not have to substantially limit a major life activity. Instead, an employee is protected under the ADA from the discrimination because of a *perceived* physical or mental impairment. In other words, even if no disability technically exists, a plaintiff's lawyer could argue that you, the employer, *regarded* the employee as having a disability and that your company therefore violated the ADA.

Finally, in preparing for any workplace discussions with your employees regarding physical or mental conditions that may be governed by the ADA, remember that the law does not merely prohibit discrimination against qualified individuals with disabilities. As alluded to above, the ADA imposes additional affirmative obligations on covered employers to provide reasonable accommodations for applicants and employees with disabilities (which may include, for example, restructuring jobs, making worksites and workstations accessible, modifying schedules, providing services such as interpreters, and modifying equipment and policies). Employers must engage in the interactive process with the employee to determine what accommodations would be reasonable.

Medical intervention may be the only practical direction in which an employer can lead an employee under these circumstances. If that's the case, it's best to allow human resources to follow the ADA process. Just be sure and close your conversation this way: "Amelia, thank you for taking the time to discuss this matter with me, and please let me know if there's anything you need from me." Assuming the problem may be due to a medical condition, it's best to follow up with human resources to make sure Amelia made an appointment with them. If not, human resources should reach out to her to start the interactive process. Remember, given your conversation with Amelia, the company may be on notice that Amelia has a disability and may require a reasonable accommodation. Accordingly, the company has to act.

Practically speaking, you'll have demonstrated care and compassion to an employee in need of your help. Legally speaking, you'll have begun the process of fulfilling the company's obligation under the ADA to engage in the interactive process with the employee to determine an appropriate accommodation, if one is applicable, resulting in a work environment that enables the individual to be comfortable and productive. Well done!

# OVERCOMING UNWILLINGNESS
# TO CONFRONT PROBLEMS HEAD-ON

Managers who avoid confrontation cause lots of angst and drama in the workplace. Small problems tend to become bigger ones if not addressed quickly, and turnover and lawsuits tend to result when perceptions of unfairness permeate the office or shop floor.

Some people are born natural leaders, while others need to develop and strengthen that ability. Whatever the case, it's in your and your company's best interests to ensure that problem issues are addressed head-on whenever possible. Sure, there will be times when a wait-and-see approach will make the most sense, but more often than not, bad habits need to be addressed early so that inappropriate behaviors don't perpetuate themselves in the workplace.

Let's look at an example. Your company prides itself on its inclusive culture. Employees are generally treated with respect, your line managers create an environment where workers have input and say into the day-to-day operations of the plant, and yelling and screaming are just not what you're all about. In steps a new hire in your sales management group who comes from the Ivan the Terrible school of "motivating" subordinates.

Before too long, the first incident gets reported about her publicly humiliating a subordinate at a staff meeting. You hear all the details about this incident from salespeople who were present at the meeting, but you hear nothing from the director of sales who reports to you and who oversees the group and ran the meeting. Patiently you wait, hoping to hear from your director, but nothing. You decide to wait and keep a close eye on the situation, only to hear about another incident of public shaming during the following week's meeting. Still, no word from your director.

Let's assume you've done your homework and received consistent feedback about both incidents from witnesses on-site. You're ready to discuss the issue with the director who, in fairness, may have addressed this with the new hire. Still, it's funny that the director didn't mention anything to you up to this point.

Chris, how are things going with your staff these days? [*Fine.*] Are there any issues that you want me to be aware of or that you need to bring to my attention? [*No.*] Oh, I see. How's your new hire doing: Olivia, the sales manager? Has her onboarding process been smooth, or does she need anything at this point? [*No. She's fine.*]

Well, it surprises me to hear that, seeing that I've heard there were "shout-outs" at her first two weekly staff meetings. People who were present came to see me to provide me with blow-by-blow details of her attacks on Bill and Ryan for not making their outbound call numbers. Why don't you tell me how things look from your vantage point?

[*Well, sure, there have been two incidents of calling to everyone's attention the fact that two members of the team weren't reaching their outbound call numbers, but I have to defer to Olivia. This is her new role, and I need her to establish accountability and establish appropriate expectations for everyone.*]

Let me ask you this: I understand what she's doing; my question is, *how* is she doing it? Has she spoken to you about her intended approach before the staff meetings, or did you simply learn of her tactics during the meetings themselves?

[*A little bit of both, I guess. She told me she planned on "drawing a little blood" at first to make sure everyone was paying attention. From that point forward, though, she said she'd take a calmer approach to managing the day-to-day operations of the sales function.*]

And once you saw how Olivia handled those meetings, Chris, were you in agreement with her methodology?

[*Again, I probably wouldn't have handled it that way myself, but I'll defer to her in terms of how she wants to manage the sales team that reports to her.*]

Okay, at this point, you've calmly approached the issue to fact-find your way to the truth, and you feel disappointed that Chris would allow new hire Olivia to trample over the staff that way. First, that's not your management style. Second, Chris knows it's not your company's culture to strip people of their dignity in front of others. Third, you're now questioning Chris's role in all of this: Is he afraid to address Olivia or somehow intimidated by her? If not, why would he allow such inappropriate managerial behavior to go unaddressed? Your response is clear and unequivocal in its intent:

Chris, I'm shocked and disappointed to hear your reaction to all this. First, you know that's not how this company operates. When we have a problem, we address it professionally and appropriately. If Olivia wasn't satisfied with Bill's and Ryan's sales results, she needed to address that with them in private one-on-one meetings. We've never been known as a company to embarrass or humiliate coworkers for any reason. If Bill and Ryan are having bad months, then Olivia should have taken the time to find out what was going on privately and behind closed doors. That's how I'd expect you to advise her as her supervisor.

Next, I'm wondering if she's going to be a fit within the organization. If her way of dealing with people is by stripping them of their dignity in front of their peers, then you've got to know that she doesn't have the style or temperament that would make for a long-term, viable employee. After all, I wouldn't want to work for a sales manager that treated me that way. Would you? [*Probably not.*]

Third, and most important, I'm questioning *your discretion and judgment here.* Why didn't you address Olivia's managerial conduct as soon as it happened? Why didn't you call her aside and let her know that although that behavior may be accepted and condoned at other companies, it has no place here? More important, why haven't you kept me in the loop as to why this has been going on? Why did I need to hear about it from your staff members instead of you? [*I'm sorry—I can see your point about addressing her and keeping you in the loop.*]

Here are my expectations, Chris, and we need to make sure we're in sync here. First, any newly hired managers with a "my-way-or-the-highway" approach to leadership should be considered mis-hires, unless they can demonstrate very quickly that they're willing to switch over to our style of leadership, communication, and respect. Second, any time there's a controversial new hire for any reason, I want to hear about it from you before I hear about it from your staff members or people from other departments.

Finally, I won't permit this sense of flying blind to continue. Likewise, I don't want a director on my staff who doesn't proactively address both the performance and conduct expectations of our employees, especially of those employees in leadership roles.

Am I clear and do these sound like reasonable expectations on my part? [*Yes.*] Good. Then you're sure you understand that I won't permit a leader on my team who avoids confrontation. [*Yes, I understand.*] And you're doubly clear that I expect you to address these types of problems head-on as soon as they occur, while keeping me abreast of the situation? [*Yes, I am now.*]

I'm happy to hear that. Now tell me how you plan on addressing Olivia's behavior in this particular case.

Phew! A tougher conversation, no doubt, but you have every right to question any subordinate who fails to keep you abreast of problems in your area or who otherwise appears to avoid confrontation at all costs.

Avoiding confrontation is one of the cardinal sins of management: be sure to break any bad habits or proclivities in your subordinates who seem to shy away from this necessary leadership discipline.

# THE CRITICAL NATURE
# OF PROGRESSIVE DISCIPLINE

## SHIFTING THE POWER PARADIGM
## BACK TO YOUR COMPANY

This section shows how to handle employee problems by implementing progressive discipline—a step-by-step process to inform an employee that his performance or behavior needs to improve or he risks termination from the company. It covers other approaches to written warnings, including writing a letter of clarification (an informal warning), offering a decision-making leave (where an employee takes a paid day off to contemplate whether she really wants to keep her job and is willing to change her behavior), and several types of "last-chance agreements." It also shows how to document discipline properly and effectively and how to avoid "pre-taliation," where an employee makes a preemptive strike against a manager to turn the tables and put the company on defense before the manager disciplines the employee. Knowing how to handle all these situations—before they occur—is the best way for managers to fortify themselves with a defensive leadership stance, which benefits managers and employees alike.

# WHAT IS PROGRESSIVE DISCIPLINE AND HOW DOES IT HELP BOTH COMPANIES AND WORKERS?

Progressive discipline is a means of communicating performance or conduct problems in a direct and timely manner so that employees can improve. It typically includes a series of documented steps that escalate if the problematic issues continue. The concepts of progressive discipline and workplace due process go hand in hand.

Workplace due process means recognizing an employee's right to be informed of unsatisfactory job performance or inappropriate workplace conduct in order to have a chance to defend himself and improve before an adverse employment action (such as discharge) is taken. This standard of fairness and equity harkens back to the founding of our nation in the eighteenth century when Americans borrowed from English law in establishing new rules to govern society.

The way due process shows itself in practice can be found in the progressive discipline paradigm—the series of notifications of problematic performance that must be corrected before termination results. "Due process" requires managers to ensure that an underperforming employee understands what the problem is, what needs to done to correct the problem, what will happen if acceptable progress doesn't occur and sustain itself, and how much time the individual has to demonstrate improvement. As a manager or corporate leader, you also need to provide employees with resources they can use to improve: coaching and commitment, training, and material resources. When your company uses progressive discipline, it's a win for both sides: you (the employer) focus on helping your workers; in turn, your workers are given specific guidance on how they can improve to meet company expectations.

## THE TRADITIONAL PROGRESSIVE DISCIPLINE PARADIGM

The traditional progressive discipline paradigm follows four steps:

1. Verbal correction (which may be documented)
2. Written warning
3. Final written warning
4. Discharge

These four steps help prove, via documentation, that you made a good-faith effort to help an underperforming employee improve at work. Your affirmative efforts to help improve your employee's performance and reset expectations must be clearly documented and reasonably achievable. Should a worker be unwilling or unable to raise performance or conduct to the expected standards outlined, then you, the employer, would be left with little choice other than to terminate. Keep in mind that you may be required to demonstrate that the discipline was meted out fairly and was consistent with your own policies so that any employee could reasonably expect to be terminated under similar circumstances.

Following are the elements of due process:

First, the employee must understand your expectations and the consequences of failing to meet your performance standards. If a write-up merely documents a performance problem without pointing to what the consequences will be if he fails to improve, the write-up will lack the "teeth" necessary to meet due process guidelines.

Second, you must be consistent in applying your organization's rules. Workers have the right to consistent and predictable employer responses when a rule is violated; you can't address problems on an ad hoc basis without being perceived as arbitrary, unreasonable, or even discriminatory. Also bear in mind that practice usually trumps policy—that is, regardless of what your handbook or policy and procedure manual says, your past practices will be scrutinized for consistency. In addition, if you fail to follow through on threatened consequences, that could damage the credibility of your disciplinary system and set an unintended precedent: for example, if your company forgives one employee for making certain mistakes, it can be argued that your company needs to forgive any or all other employees for making those same or similar errors.

Third, the discipline must be appropriate for the offense. If an employee performs poorly occasionally or commits a minor transgression, you *can* take action, but those situations are probably not cause for terminating that employee. You need to consider an employee's overall performance track record and prior disciplinary history.

Fourth, your company should generally meet with an employee first and give the individual an opportunity to respond before issuing disciplinary warnings. Administering discipline without allowing employees to share their side of the story is begging for trouble. Likewise, be sure to include a section on your disciplinary warning template that invites employee feedback and/or rebuttal.

Unfortunately, many companies don't offer these self-defense principles to employees in their approach to corrective action.

Fifth, you need to give the employee a reasonable period of time to improve her performance. Otherwise, your disciplinary actions will appear to be an artificial excuse to terminate the employee.

Several other rules of thumb are important to bear in mind as well when dealing with workplace due process:

- As an employer, you have the right to change your policies at any time. Simply give your employees advance notice of the change, along with its effective date, so that all workers can ready themselves to meet your newly defined expectations.

- Infractions need not be treated identically but should be treated consistently. For example, occasional versus habitual tardiness will typically invoke a different response from the company. In other words, you're not precluded from disciplining Emma who reports to work late regularly just because you didn't discipline Tyler who came in late one day last week. Likewise, sleeping on the job can be a significant infraction, but it's certainly less of an issue for a secretary (who may receive a written warning for a first offense) than for a night shift nurse (whose first offense results in a final written warning) or for an anesthesiologist (who is terminated for falling asleep during a medical procedure).

- The *final incident* plays a particularly significant role in determining how to best respond to any infraction: a clean and compelling final incident, in breach of previous documented warnings, makes for a much safer termination if your company is challenged later.

Progressive discipline usually progresses when there is a repeated violation of the same rule or type of rule: for example, repeated lateness or unexcused absences. There should generally be a link between events in order to move to the next stage: without this, you could end up with a series of independent verbal warnings rather than a *progression* from a verbal to a written to a final written warning.

For example, Brandon doesn't come in to work one day and doesn't call in to explain why he isn't coming in, thus violating your organization's attendance policy; then, a week later, Brandon misses a deadline on a project. In this scenario, you could give him two separate verbal warnings because these are independent and unrelated transgressions. In contrast, suppose Tiara doesn't come to work or call in to explain why (just as Brandon did), but Tiara then starts coming to work late regularly. In this case, Tiara will progress through the discipline system because both her transgressions are intrinsically connected: her unauthorized absences and lateness have a negative effect on the workflow of your office.

Also, it is not uncommon to have an employee on separate paths of discipline. For example, suppose Leo is a shipping clerk already on final written warning for insubordination; if Leo also starts coming in late to his shift, that shouldn't necessarily be cause for terminating Leo, because lateness is a problem generally unrelated to insubordination. Therefore, you can't use Leo's new problem as the proverbial "straw that breaks the camel's back" to justify terminating him, because there is no interrelationship between his lateness and his insubordination. Lateness interferes with workflow, whereas insubordination relates to individual behavior and conduct—which is a separate problem altogether.

On the other hand, because insubordination is a conduct infraction, any other behavior or conduct infractions during the active period of the write-up may indeed result in dismissal. For example, if you've given Leo a final written warning for his insubordination, and he suddenly engages in antagonistic behavior toward his co-workers, insults a customer, or refuses to follow a supervisor's instructions, then a discharge determination could be warranted (barring any significant mitigating circumstances, of course).

A final point: using progressive discipline does not preclude you from firing someone on the spot, although you may have difficulty defending your actions in a wrongful termination claim. If you've denied an employee due process, the technical merits of your arguments may be largely ignored.

On the other hand, you don't have to offer progressive discipline to someone who breaks the law. Progressive discipline is an employee benefit. If an employee engages in illegal activity or other egregious conduct (such as gross insubordination, gross negligence, theft, embezzlement, time-card fraud, or drug use on company premises), you've probably got a clear shot at a quick and defensible termination (known as a *summary dismissal*, which is discussed in more detail in part 3).

To be on the safe side, speak with a labor attorney to fully explore the ramifications of such a dismissal. You want to ensure you haven't overlooked anything. If you need extra time, you can always place the worker on investigatory leave with pay pending further review and a final decision.

# DISCIPLINING AND TERMINATING PROBATIONARY WORKERS

**M**ost employers know they have a right to terminate new hires during a probationary or introductory period. But the probationary period is often misunderstood because it differs depending on whether an organization has union or at-will employees. To protect your company from unnecessary legal challenges stemming from this misunderstanding, here's a bit of background you should know.

Historically, union contracts allow for probationary periods—initial hiring periods of thirty to ninety days when companies have an undisputed right to terminate new hires without facing a grievance related to the termination, subject, of course, to the laws that protect against discrimination based on a protected classification (for example, race, gender, and the like). Because the union has waived any right to grieve the employment action, the company's only obligation is to notify the union of the termination because there's no obligation of due process or union negotiation. The collective bargaining agreement provides the employer with a contractual right to pull the plug pretty much at any time within that probationary period. (Of course, once the probationary period expires, the union will argue that a termination-for-just-cause standard will apply, meaning employees may not be terminated unless the company can establish that it had good cause for dismissal.)

In contrast, nonunion, at-will employees are not governed by collective bargaining agreements and do not have a set time window in which termination can occur without challenge. Whether or not the company has an initial probationary or introductory period, a terminated at-will employee may sue a company for wrongful termination, even if that termination occurs within the initial probationary or introductory period. Therefore, you have to be careful not to overly rely on probationary periods when terminating at-will workers. Rather, you should still actively manage and even progressively discipline employees during probationary periods to support a termination decision. You also should still vet your decision in advance through human resources or with appropriate legal counsel. If done incorrectly, the legal concept of *employment at will* may be countered by the concept of *sue at will*! So, be cautious about your right to terminate at-will employees "at whim" while within the initial introductory period.

Of course, if your company hires employees at will to begin with, there's really little need for a probationary period. After all, in an at-will environment, the employee can be terminated at any time, with or without cause or notice. A probationary period allows that same relationship only for an initial thirty to ninety days.

So why would a company institute a probationary period for a few months when the entire employment relationship is theoretically governed by that same premise? The answer is simple: companies are accustomed to this union vestige, which continues to be passed down from generation to generation. In other cases, organizations have become enamored with the psychological comfort that probation periods provide. Whatever the reason, many employment lawyers consequently argue that there's no reason for a probation period in an at-will environment because it's overkill. More problematically, the existence of a probation period may infer that a company that allows employees to continue to work beyond their probation period may create an expectation that workers are entitled to some greater right to job security in the form of workplace due process than they had while in their probation periods.

The topic of probationary periods in union versus nonunion environments goes beyond the scope of this book. But it's important that you understand this brief history to ensure that you handle this topic appropriately in your termination conversations with new hires. If nothing else, remember this: terminating an at-will probationary employee still carries legal risk, and you may want to occasionally provide some form of workplace due process (typically in the form of a written warning) even to new hires in their probation periods. It never hurts to provide a written warning as an insurance policy should that individual choose to sue your company for wrongful probationary termination.

It is highly recommended that you do not include any type of severance or separation pay with new hires in their probation period. Although many companies try to smooth the blow of the termination by paying out an additional two weeks' worth of wages, a plaintiff's attorney looking to sue may very well attribute negative motives toward your benign and well-intentioned gesture. In short, your "payoff" money could be seen as hush or guilt money, paid out to entice the individual to go away quietly. No good deed goes unpunished, and many unsuspecting employers have been blindsided by such manipulative interpretations by plaintiffs' attorneys.

That a company has a probationary period makes it easier to explain the termination without written warnings. If your company doesn't have a probationary period, it would be just as simple to replace the probationary period concept with the employment-at-will concept—that is, "Because our employees are hired at will, we do not have an obligation to go through the steps of progressive discipline in the form of written warnings and the like." (Technically, this may be true, but understand that it is very much in your company's best interests to apply progressive discipline in the majority of cases, even during probation periods. After all, a written warning, even during a probation period, can only help and will rarely hurt your case. Looking at this another way, it can never hurt to provide extra workplace due process.)

As always, remember to treat the individual with dignity and respect, remain available should he have follow-up questions or requests, and keep the tenor and tone of your conversation businesslike yet caring.

## A SPECIAL NOTE ABOUT THE TIMING OF TERMINATION MEETINGS

Make it a practice to terminate early in the day and early in the week so that you're available to meet or speak with a terminated individual who has questions. Terminating on Friday afternoons at five is a practice that you should avoid because it leaves terminated employees with no resources or human contact to turn to when they may be feeling vulnerable or in need.

# 13

# WHY IS IT SO HARD FOR LEADERS TO APPLY PROGRESSIVE DISCIPLINE?

In today's legal system, companies that discharge employees will, if challenged, need to prove they made affirmative efforts to rehabilitate those employees before reaching the ultimate decision to terminate. When confronted by an arbitrator or scrutinized by a jury, companies need to show they had no alternative but to separate an individual who refused to accept the organization's invitations to improve his or her performance. Without such proof, the company can find itself liable to the former employee for back pay, job reinstatement, and, potentially, punitive damages. To make matters worse, those punitive damages could in certain circumstances be levied against the manager personally, depending on the state in which the manager works and the theory of relief asserted against the manager.

When confronting employees regarding their performance or behavior, many managers have the following concerns:

- How will the employee take the news?
- Will confrontation make matters worse?

- ■ What if the employee improves only long enough to get past the active time frame of the disciplinary write-up?
- ■ Also, because the write-up is a legal document, there is a residual fear that what you put in writing can somehow come back to haunt you. For example, managers typically second-guess themselves when it comes to questions like these:
  - ❑ Can I write specifics?
  - ❑ Am I violating this individual's privacy?
  - ❑ Is the employee's problem somehow protected by one of the many worker protection laws like the Family Medical Leave Act (FMLA), the Americans with Disabilities Act (ADA), or workers' comp discrimination rulings?
  - ❑ What if there are numerous problems that don't seem to be related to one another—can I move forward in the progressive discipline process by somehow bundling those disparate infractions together?

Managers have come to fear addressing even minor performance shortcomings until they become major impediments. By that time, the problems typically get so out of control that managers reactively initiate the disciplinary process in order to build a "paper trail" for a case against an employee as rapidly as possible. What magnificent advantages lie ahead for managers armed with the tools to proactively address minor concerns before they become major ones!

As an HR practitioner and university instructor, I've seen firsthand how companies go through the agony of reinstating poor performers with back wages and reintegrating those individuals into departments that have long since "healed" from the original terminations. I've also seen damage awards that defy logic as well as workers' compensation "cumulative trauma" claims that can take years to settle. And although no system can guarantee that a company will win every wrongful termination challenge, a well written disciplinary warning that invites employees to involve themselves in their own improvement game plan and that clearly outlines the company's expectations and affirmative efforts at helping those employees better themselves will go a long way toward fending off litigators' attacks and mitigating damage award settlements.

Yes, progressive discipline can be confrontational, even under the best of circumstances. But progressive discipline is often successful at turning around performance and conduct challenges so that employees can keep their jobs and organizations can avoid ending up in the litigation arena. No one wants to be disciplined, of course, but once the intervention occurs—especially if done with the individual's best interests in mind and coupled with appropriate training—the problem often disappears. Even if it doesn't, it provides your organization with a solid defense against wrongful termination and discrimination claims because "good faith personnel actions" are just that—an opportunity to help turn around a problematic situation or wayward performer. Progressive discipline, when done correctly, helps employees, their managers, and the organization. As an employment intervention, it can work wonders on the employee and limit corporate liability. What more can you ask? Simply stated, all corporate leaders need to master this critical tool and add it to their tool kit.

# PREVENTING MISTAKES
# WHEN DOCUMENTING DISCIPLINE

When documenting disciplinary actions about an employee, it's important to know—and prevent—two of the biggest mistakes that employers make.

First, many employers give themselves extra hurdles to jump through by documenting "state of mind" offenses. In an attempt to demonstrate an employee's carelessness or lack of discretion, employers will use qualifying terms and adverbs like *willfully, deliberately, recklessly, purposely,* and *intentionally.* This may help them communicate the depth of their dissatisfaction with the employee's substandard performance or conduct, but it may create an additional burden of proof if they are forced to substantiate their contentions. After all, how could you, the employer, know that an employee did something willfully or intentionally? In general, ensure that your disciplinary documentation is objective, stemming from observation. Remove any potential pitfalls by appearing to judge the employee's intentions, as judgmental accusations have no place in the progressive discipline arena. Therefore, you should avoid mental element qualifiers as much as possible so that you don't have to prove an employee's state of mind at the time a particular offense was committed.

Second, many employers fail to realize that disciplinary documentation is legally discoverable and may be used against them by a current or former employee. For example, if you state, "Your failure to properly [execute some task] *has compromised* an entire pool of mortgage loans," then you are codifying the damage done to the banking institution. That disciplinary document, in the wrong hands, could very easily become a leveraging point to substantiate a plaintiff's claim for damages (in this case, from investors in the firm's stock).

This becomes even more important in sexual harassment claims. Of course, if an employee engages in activities that, in your opinion, create a hostile or offensive working environment, then you'll want to impress upon him the seriousness of his actions. But if you state, "You have created a hostile and offensive working environment," that discoverable document could be used by a plaintiff's attorney as clear evidence that harassment did indeed occur.

Likewise, don't title the subject of a progressive disciplinary document "Sexual Harassment," as "sexual harassment" is considered a legal conclusion: a plaintiff's attorney could use it to demonstrate proof that the harassment occurred. Instead, make the title something like "Violation of Policy 360.42—Creating and Sustaining a Friendly and Inclusive Work Environment" or something similar. The documentation should not appear to codify in any way that harassment actually occurred.

To remedy these potential pitfalls, you're best off stating, "Your failure to properly [execute some task] *could have compromised* an entire pool of loans," or "Your actions *suggest that* a hostile and offensive working environment *could have* been created." Likewise,

"Your actions *appear to* violate Policy 360.42—Creating and Sustaining a Friendly and Inclusive Work Environment." This way, the responsible disciplinary action that you took won't as easily be misinterpreted as confirmation that wrongdoing actually occurred. Be careful not to let your own documentation incriminate you.

15

# AVOIDING EMPLOYEE "PRETALIATION" AGAINST UNSUSPECTING MANAGERS AND SUPERVISORS

Leading defensively requires managers in the current corporate environment to be more aware of how sophisticated workers have become in using the legal system against their companies. In addition, you need to acknowledge that you can't do this alone— you've got an affirmative obligation to disclose certain matters to HR, your boss, the legal department, an ombudsman, or some other compliance officer when certain facts arise that require assistance from a third party, impartial observer, and witness. Finally, you need to create a record—both verbally and in writing—to ensure that the company is positioned in the best light possible should litigation later arise.

Statistically, one in four managers will become involved in some form of employment-related litigation during their careers, and that's an awfully high percentage, especially if you live outside of high-litigation states like California or New York. Therefore, your ability to spot problem issues, escalate them appropriately, and resolve them fairly on the spot or prepare the appropriate record for litigation becomes a critical leadership attribute that, once mastered, will benefit you for the rest of your career.

Workers are sophisticated consumers, and whether they figure this out on their own or get tips from plaintiffs' attorneys coaching them on the sidelines, just waiting for the person to get fired so they could initiate litigation, it's your responsibility to spot issues and involve the appropriate internal parties to support you from the very beginning. For example, suppose an employee is afraid she's going to be fired or suspects that her boss is somehow out to get her. She may reach out to a lawyer to see if she has any legal protections, and that's where plaintiff lawyers' advice and counsel can get really interesting: "Well, I probably can't help you until the company takes some adverse action against you, such as termination, but let me ask you this: Do you know who your internal HR representatives are? Have you spoken with them about your problem, and if so, what did they say?" This question seems fairly straightforward and benign, the assumption being that the employee should try to resolve the matter internally with HR before hiring an attorney to sue the company.

But there's more to this question than meets the eye: in many instances, attorneys instruct a potential plaintiff client (such as your employee) to initiate a "preemptive strike" against the manager by complaining about the manager's conduct *before* the manager has a chance to take further punitive action regarding the employee's performance. The result of such "pretaliation" is that workers who are performing poorly can potentially "reverse engineer" the record and put the company on the defensive. With that record in place, it becomes much more difficult for the company to terminate the individual because such actions may appear to be retaliatory. Here's what it looks like in chronological order:

1. An employee senses she's about to be disciplined or terminated for substandard job performance and reaches out to an attorney for help.

2.  The attorney encourages the employee to complain to HR about the manager's conduct, specifically using words like *hostile work environment*, *harassment*, *intimidation*, *bullying*, or *retaliation*.

3.  The company has a more difficult time terminating the employee due to the recent harassment claim that the employee initiated against the manager.

4.  The plaintiff's attorney wins either way: if the termination is delayed for the time being, a strong trust builds between the lawyer and the client because the attorney gave great advice that benefited the client; if the termination goes through, the attorney has another arrow in her quiver to shoot back at the company in the litigation phase in the form of retaliation.

You, the manager, may be acting in good faith in disciplining this employee only to find yourself the target of an investigation from HR because of the employee's complaint.

This situation occurs again and again in corporate offices, with managers inadvertently stepping on land mines and not realizing until after the fact that a bomb went off.

Here's how you'll know when this situation is at hand: HR receives an employee complaint about a manager's conduct and calls a meeting with the manager and the manager's boss. The HR person opens the meeting by saying, "Joe, we've received a complaint of harassment from one of your employees regarding how you manage them, and we need to explain the nature of the complaint and also to learn your side of the story."

The manager asks who lodged the complaint and is told it was Heidi Jones. He becomes furious and replies, "It was Heidi? You've got to be kidding! I was just about to come to HR to discuss placing her on a final written warning because she's such a poor performer. She comes in late, leaves early, and . . ."

*Boom!* The land mine just exploded. The employee—either on her own or under an attorney's guidance—figured out that by launching her claim first about her boss's conduct, she could turn the tables on the record that was being created regarding her performance. She engineered a perfect scenario for a retaliation claim later, and the manager didn't even see it coming.

The lesson? Don't fall prey to a preemptive strike. When your gut tells you there's a problem with someone's performance or you sense the person may be speaking with a lawyer, contact HR right away. After all, whoever gets to HR first gets the ball rolling in terms of how HR conducts its investigation: If you initiate the matter with HR and focus on your subordinate's substandard *performance*, then HR moves in one direction. But if the employee meets with HR first to complain about your *conduct*, then HR moves in a different direction in terms of opening an investigation surrounding potential managerial misconduct. Timing, it turns out, is one of the most critical elements in determining what type of record is made in many employment-related situations.

Finally, don't manage by fear of a lawsuit. Lawsuits are part of the cost of doing business in corporate America from time to time, and managing by fear rarely has positive results. Instead, just be sure that if a lawsuit comes your way, you're getting sued on your terms rather than theirs. The most successful way to do this is to act professionally, demonstrate respect for those you supervise, and enlist the services of internal support teams (such as HR) that are there to help you through these very types of situations. It's okay to take things "outside the family" and partner with HR when your gut intuition is telling you that something may be amiss. Always consider the record that is being created, and get that hot potato off your lap and share it with the department responsible for engaging in these very activities—HR. (If your organization doesn't have an HR department, bring the matter immediately to your supervisor's attention and seek the support of your internal legal counsel or external law firm.) You'll find that a winning strategy like this will allow you to thrive in your career without any of the angst, drama, or histrionics that plague certain managers who opt to go it alone or refuse help.

# DOCUMENTATION TECHNIQUES AND STRATEGIES

INCIDENT DESCRIPTIONS, PERFORMANCE IMPROVEMENT
PLANS, AND OUTCOMES AND CONSEQUENCES

**D**ocumentation techniques and strategies are critical to understand because much of corrective action is actually driven by the template your organization uses to notify the employee of the problem, reset expectations going forward, and outline the consequences of failure to improve. Unfortunately, most organizations don't do a particularly thorough job when issuing documented corrective action. The content is either woefully lacking in terms of providing specific details of what occurred and the negative organizational consequences that resulted or else the write-up fails to demonstrate the outcomes and consequences that might justify termination. Let's look at the three key sections of a write-up template so you understand philosophically what employers are trying to accomplish in terms of outlining the problems that exist (that is, incident descriptions), helping workers assume responsibility for their actions (via performance improvement plans, or PIPs), and including consequence language that will withstand legal scrutiny (that is, outcomes).

*Incident Descriptions.* Issuing progressive discipline isn't supposed to feel like giving someone a parking ticket. It's not simply a matter of checking a box or writing a one-liner that reads, "Andrew failed to dispense the proper medication and the appropriate dosage," and leaving it at that. Instead, refer to the writing tools you learned in high school: who, what, where, when, why, and how belong in the narrative. This way, the employee has a clear understanding of what happened to whom at what time and what location. Using the sentence above as an introduction, the follow-up might read:

> Specifically, at 10:07 PM on January 10 in the Bone Marrow Transplant Unit's L-Wing, Andrew erroneously dispensed 1,000 mg of Tylenol rather than 4,000 mg of acetaminophen to Patient #654321, as required under the patient's care plan. Although the patient did not notice the difference or suffer physically from the error, the substitution of medications could have compromised the patient's overall care and created a safety risk.

With details outlined so specifically, the employee can recall and discuss the specifics of the incident, defend himself if he disagrees with his supervisor's findings, and most important, learn from the mistake now that it has been brought to his attention in such detail. Further, notice the documentation of the potential organizational impact: "the substitution of medications could have compromised the patient's overall care and created a safety risk." It's this negative organization impact that justifies the disciplinary action.

Similarly, when it comes to describing an employee's "bad attitude," you are responsible for painting a picture with words such that an independent judge or arbitrator could picture the scenario clearly, even a year later when the matter was reexamined as a factor leading up to the employee's termination. For example:

Jasmine, when I asked you about the status of update on the Samuels project during our staff meeting on May 30, you rolled your eyes, harrumphed, put your hands on your hips, and responded in a sharp tone, "Why is that even being brought up? It's a small project for a tiny client; the contact over there barely returns our calls, and last I looked, they'd fallen behind on their scheduled payments. I haven't looked into it because I'm too busy working on other, *real* projects for clients who pay their bills. They'll have to wait until I have time to follow up on the matter." Further, you shared your comments in a loud and sarcastic voice in front of the rest of the team, which made me and others feel uncomfortable because of your disrespectful and flippant tone. I remind you that all clients are important to our company's and our team's success. You do not have the discretion to pick and choose your clients or projects or justify your failure to follow up with the people at Samuels without informing me of any problems you are having with them communication-wise.

Again, incident descriptions must be able to stand on their own and paint a picture of the employee's substandard job performance or inappropriate workplace conduct so that a stranger reading the content six months or a year later could understand the employer's reasoning behind the discipline. Clarity in your writing and documentation of the negative organizational impact are critical elements of progressive discipline, both for fairness and legal compliance reasons.

*Performance Improvement Plans (PIPs).* PIPs set go-forward expectations so that the employee clearly understands what's expected in terms of acceptable performance and appropriate conduct. As such, including a section in your disciplinary documentation that reads "Going forward, I expect you to . . ." or "In the future, you are expected to . . ." helps the individual understand in no uncertain terms what will be necessary to fix the situation at hand and avoid future discipline.

The PIP section also provides employers with an opportunity to document what they're willing to do to proactively rehabilitate the worker. Workers often shift blame to employers, claiming that the company failed to train them properly for discriminatory reasons when employees don't master the work at hand. To avoid such claims, and to be as transparent as possible in terms of your attempts to help the individual turn things around, document your efforts at helping the employee master the problem. For example, scheduling the worker to take a refresher course on company time and at company expense at a local junior college goes a long way in ensuring a perception of fairness on the employer's part.

Likewise, documenting your willingness to meet with the individual one-on-one every Monday morning in your office from ten to ten thirty over the next three weeks demonstrates your efforts in ensuring that the individual understands the key elements of her job. If your company has a learning management system, identify particular videos that may have to do with customer care and client management and assign them within the PIP section of the warning. Sometimes, it's as easy as providing a copy of a company policy (for example, attendance and tardiness) and attaching that document to the warning in an effort to demonstrate your willingness to help. Some organizations even provide contact information for their Employee Assistance Program (EAP) in case the worker needs to speak with someone privately. Whatever the case, it's critical not only to clarify expectations but to likewise engage in the employee's turnaround by providing appropriate training and resources.

Finally, your template should provide a section that invites employees to rebut the document or share their own ideas for improving the situation at hand. True, it may potentially invite disagreement or refusal to assume responsibility for a problem. More often, though, it gives individuals control over the matter at hand and encourages them to meet the employer halfway by doing their part to turn things around. Besides, as an employer, you always want to know the employee's side of the story before the matter proceeds to litigation. Simply add a section to the PIP that states: "I recognize you may have certain suggestions for improving the situation at hand. Therefore, I encourage you to provide your own input and suggestions and/or rebuttal on a separate sheet of paper if you wish."

Note that if an employee writes a rebuttal, that worker should have the last word. Employers should not "rebut rebuttals" or otherwise engage in a paper chase. The warning stands, the employee's rebuttal is well noted and added to the warning, and both sides can agree to disagree. (There can be an exception, of course, if new information is introduced that needs to be reflected in the record.) The broader goal, however, in treating employees with respect when issuing progressive discipline lies in welcoming them back to the fold by extending tools and resources to help them succeed. More often than not, such interventions succeed; when not, the documentation at the very least insulates your organization from wrongful termination liability by mitigating potential damages that may be levied against your company.

*Outcomes and Consequences.* The optimal language to include at the end of the documented verbal, written, or final written warning states: "Failure to demonstrate immediate and sustained improvement may result in further disciplinary action, up to and including termination of employment." Such language is incontestable in its intent. It is specific regarding expectations and consequences, which supports the due process elements of ensuring that the employee was treated fairly throughout the process and understood what the consequences of inaction would be if improvement is not attained.

## AVOID VAGUE "CONSEQUENCE" LANGUAGE

A note of caution: Many employers mistakenly leave this sentence out altogether or make reference to vague consequences like, "If this situation does not improve, serious consequences may result." When they then move to termination, the plaintiff attorney defending your ex-employee has a field day littering the court with questions like: "What did you mean by *serious consequences*? Should my client have recognized that her job was in immediate jeopardy of being lost because you alluded to *serious consequences*? Would you be surprised if I told you that my client, your ex-employee, assumed that *serious consequences* meant that she'd be disciplined further? She was totally denied due process because she was confused by your documented reference to *serious consequences* and didn't realize her job was in jeopardy. How would you have reasonably expected her to know that at the time?" In short, don't let your documentation put the focus on you and come back to bite your company: employ the recommended language above so that employees have a clear understanding that termination may result.

# AN ALTERNATIVE TO FORMAL CORRECTIVE ACTION

## "LETTERS OF CLARIFICATION"

**M**any managers wonder whether there is a way to communicate their dissatisfaction with an employee's performance or conduct without resorting to formal discipline. The answer is *yes*: formal discipline is only one method of proactively rehabilitating workers by focusing their efforts on changed behaviors or heightened performance. It's often the case that an informal "counseling session"—typically the first natural step in the communication process—will work wonders and fix the problem right from the start.

On the other hand, if the initial verbal counseling session doesn't bring about the desired results, a letter of clarification may be just what's needed. For example, suppose you're a hospital administrator and you have a problem with one of the nursing assistants who is responsible for pulling patients' charts and transporting patients in wheelchairs. Several weeks after notifying her verbally about a problem with her work, you're not satisfied with the level of commitment and patient focus that she appears to be exercising. You notice the same apathetic behaviors setting in again: Kiara is not returning medical files, she's not using the department's magnetic scoreboard to show when she's out of the office, and then a patient complains about Kiara sitting her in a wheelchair wet from the rain.

Is it time for a formal written warning, or are you afraid that might be too harsh since the infractions are fairly minor? Well, fear not. You no longer need to choose either verbal coaching or formal progressive discipline because a third option is available: a letter of clarification might be just the right tool to impress on Kiara the seriousness of her infractions. Letters of clarification are presented to the employee in written format and require the employee's signature. Logically, when things are written down, they are perceived to be more serious.

In addition, when employees sign their names to documents related to their performance or conduct, they develop a healthy sense of paranoia that those documents may be used later down the line to establish some pattern of past history in their actions. That's what progressive discipline is all about:

■ Showing employees what is wrong with their performance or conduct
■ Telling them what they need to do to fix the problem at hand
■ Giving them a reasonable amount of time to fix the problem
■ Clearly documenting the consequences of failing to meet your expectations

The letter of clarification will accomplish the first three (positive) goals of progressive discipline without having the sting of the fourth element of consequences—language along the lines of "further disciplinary action, up to and including termination."

In fact, letters of clarification should specifically state that they are not disciplinary documents. As such, they don't carry the heavy stigma of "being written up." Here's what Kiara's letter of clarification looks like:

Kiara, over the past three weeks, I've shared with you my concerns regarding your performance and conduct. Specifically, I've told you that you are not handling patients' files correctly because items are being misfiled and files are being left in the office without being returned to the central filing area. In addition, a patient complained that you delivered a wheelchair that was still wet from the rain to the patient pickup area. Finally, you have failed on several occasions to use the magnetic location board to show when you were on break or lunch. As a result, the schedulers were not able to locate you in a timely fashion.

This isn't a disciplinary document, Kiara. It will not be placed in your formal personnel file and will not be shared with other members of management at this time. *But I have put my concerns in writing to impress upon you the seriousness of these multiple smaller errors.* My greatest concern lies in the fact that you appear less focused on your work now than at any time in the past five years. You also appear to be apathetic about the outcome of your assignments, and several of your coworkers have shared concerns with me as well regarding changes in your work patterns.

I want you to know that I'm here to help you in any way I can. On the other hand, I am holding you fully accountable for meeting all hospital expectations regarding performance and conduct. I recognize that you may have certain ideas to improve the situation at hand. Therefore, I encourage you to provide your own suggestions and recommendations on paper and welcome your additional input if you would like to discuss this further. However, I hope these concerns—now in written form—impress upon you the growing seriousness of the problems at hand.

Please sign this document to evidence not only that you received it but also that you agree to accept full responsibility for fixing these issues and changing the perception problems that exist. I know you can do it, and I'm here to support you. Thank you.

X _____

    Employee Signature                         Date

Could this document later be used to justify formal disciplinary action if the employee fails to demonstrate acceptable improvement? Absolutely! A documented letter of clarification can easily be attached to a formal written disciplinary notice as proof that the matter was addressed in the past. Consequently, this letter could help strengthen a future case since you would have provided the employee with ample notification—both informally and formally—that her performance was substandard. As such, it would be much harder for a plaintiff attorney to successfully argue that you've denied the employee workplace due process. More significantly, the employee will hopefully view your handling of the matter more fairly and reasonably since you initially addressed these matters outside the formal disciplinary system.

So, when's the best time to use such informal letters? Either when individual infractions are repetitive and fairly minor in nature (like Kiara's case above) or when group infractions need to be remedied quickly. In another example, if you learn that several of your line managers are sharing employment-related references regarding past workers, then a verbal announcement to the staff may not be enough to show how serious you are about fixing the problem. Still, writing everyone up wouldn't make sense since following the "no references" policy hasn't been formally enforced in the past. Your best bet? Try a letter of clarification like this:

TO ALL ENGINEERING STAFF:

Company policy strictly prohibits providing prospective employers with reference information on past workers. All requests for references must be forwarded to human resources. Human resources will then provide the former workers' dates of employment and last title held.

Subjective references that reveal information about past workers' performance, character, or work habits—especially if negative—could expose our organization to claims of defamation and other legal damages. Since any managers who provide such references could be named individually in a lawsuit arising from such claims, it is critical that you all conform to this existing policy. Thank you.

I agree not to release any reference-checking information to any outside employers, employment agencies, or search firms, and I will forward all future calls to human resources.

X _____

　　　　Employee Signature　　　　　　　　　　　　　Date

When issuing such group clarification letters, always require that employees individually sign separate documents. Advise them that you will keep their signed letters in your department file for future reference. That should cement in their minds the commitment you've made and they've now made to following company policy and placing a particular rule "back on the front burner." If further violations occur, however, that signed document will also establish clear grounds for further disciplinary measures.

Letters of clarification, viewed by many employees as precursors to formal discipline, have the same prophylactic effect as formal discipline without the negative trappings. Added to your performance management toolbox, this alternative could strengthen communications by clarifying your expectations and, more important, involving employees in their own rehabilitation by treating them with dignity and respect.

## SPECIAL NOTE

Letters of clarification are tools that can be used occasionally when formal discipline isn't yet warranted but the employee doesn't appear to be taking your verbal admonishments seriously enough. Be careful, however, not to always issue such letters before formally disciplining employees. Otherwise, you might inadvertently create a practice of "no discipline until you've received a letter of clarification," which is neither the purpose of the tool nor the goal of its implementation.

# DECISION-MAKING LEAVES
# AND DAYS OF CONTEMPLATION

## DRAMATIC TURNAROUNDS WITHOUT A LOT OF DRAMA

One of the greatest workplace challenges for supervisors and managers lies in turning workers around when their conduct or behavior consistently disappoints you. A "decision-making leave," also known as a "day of contemplation," can often help employees realize how negatively they're coming across—without you, the employer, having to play the bad guy. Usually, the events that typically trigger the need for a decision-making leave revolve around employee conduct (as opposed to performance or attendance). In most cases, you, the manager, want the individual's behavior to change, not only for your sake and your staff's but also for the good of the employee as well.

Decision-making leaves typically come into play in scenarios like these:

1. A problematic employee with special circumstances (in this case, family ties to someone in senior management) consistently comes close to breaching a formal company policy but never quite violates it, thereby avoiding formal progressive discipline but upsetting everyone around him in

the process. Here, you want to break this employee's persistent poor habits by getting him to assume responsibility for the problem at hand and stop the roller-coaster effect of his behavior—without upsetting the senior executive family member.

2. A top sales producer who performs his job well believes he can do whatever he wants because he "can't be touched" as long as he's the best performer in the group. Here, this employee has the situation only half right: he's responsible for both his performance *and* his conduct, and he needs to understand that performing well but failing to create an inclusive work environment or fostering a sense of teamwork leaves him failing overall; if he's meeting only the performance standards but not the conduct expectations, he's coming in at 50 percent—a failing score in most organizations.

3. A long-tenured employee is due a greater amount of workplace due process because of her tenure, and you want to add a decision-making leave to her final written warning to impress on her that her position is now in immediate jeopardy of being lost. Here, your goal is to help this employee understand the severity of the situation and also to protect your organization legally, because the "three strikes and you're out" method of workplace due process doesn't necessarily work as well for long-term employees where courts may reasonably rule that you owe the individual more notice than a few simple documented warnings.

The decision-making leave is a paid day off when an employee causing lots of grief is granted the opportunity to rethink his commitment to working at your company. Unlike a formal suspension, it isn't necessarily a step in your company's documented progressive disciplinary process (but it can be, as in the third example above). Also, unlike a traditional suspension, the employee's pay is not docked for the time away from work. The worker actually *gets paid to stay home* for a day and mull over whether working for your company is the right long-term career move for him.

If this sounds like too lenient a strategy that lets the worker "benefit from being bad," don't be too quick to judge how effective this tool can actually work in the workplace. Here's why: when you treat people like adults, they typically respond in kind. Unlike formal discipline, which tends to punish workers for substandard job performance or inappropriate workplace conduct, decision-making leaves are much subtler. They provide time to self-reflect, to internalize the problem, and hopefully assume responsibility for fixing it. Also important, they give the individual a taste of unemployment—sitting at home for a day without work responsibilities—to consider their career options. As such, there's little sense of resentment toward the employer and a greater sense of accountability. Following is what a decision-making leave discussion might sound like.

> Ashley, let's talk. The issues that we've verbally addressed don't seem to be working, and I suspect you're just not taking this as seriously as you otherwise should. We're going to try something new. Tomorrow, I'm directing that you stay home for the day. You'll be paid just as if you're at work, so you don't have to worry about that. But I want you to experience what's known as a decision-making leave or a day of contemplation where you get to really think about whether you want to work here or not. There's no judgment either way, and I'll support you if you choose to remain employed with us or if you decide to resign.

While you're home, I really want you to think about whether our organization is right for you at this point and time in your career. I also want you to reflect on the experience your coworkers and our department are having with some of the challenges you've posed that we're still attempting to address. If you decide to resign, simply come in tomorrow morning at your regular start time and meet with me to share your letter of resignation. You can make tomorrow your last day or tender two weeks' notice, whatever you prefer. Again, I'll support you in any way I can, including if you choose to go this route.

On the other hand, if you decide you want to keep this job and remain with us, then you'll have a homework assignment tomorrow while you're off. (Remember, I'm paying you for the day.) In that case, you need to draft a letter to my attention acknowledging the challenges we've experienced together, along with your commitment to fix the perception problem at hand. This commitment letter won't be placed in your personnel file—I'll keep it in my office. But if some form of progressive discipline becomes necessary in the future because these issues remain problematic, then the commitment letter that you wrote to me will be attached to the disciplinary warning that you receive at the time.

My goal is to treat you like an adult, demonstrate respect for you and the position you hold, but end the roller coaster of issues that we've been discussing over the past few months. Do you understand now why I'm doing this and what the goal is? [*Yes.*] Good. Why don't you repeat it for me so we're both on the same page? [*I get to spend the day home tomorrow with pay and rethink my commitment to this company and whether I want to continue working here. I have two choices: come in the next day with a letter of resignation or deliver a letter to you assuming responsibility for the problems we've been having and committing to eliminate them going forward.*]

Well said. You've captured the whole purpose of the decision-making leave very accurately. Do you have any questions at this point? [*No, but I've never heard of anything like this before and I feel really bad that you feel the need to do this with me.*] I understand. This is totally private—no one else will know. I'm just hoping that you realize all the good things that exist here, but I also have to respect that timing plays an important role in people's lives, so sometimes staying isn't always the ideal thing. Whatever the case, I'm here to support you. I want for you what you want for you. Let's catch up the day after tomorrow so we can discuss your decision.

This element of holding people accountable without issuing corrective action or negatively impacting their pay tends to trigger a higher sense of awareness in the form of "healthy guilt" rather than an anger response. *Anger* is external, and if you, the big bad employer, discipline workers and deduct their wages for any reason, they'll become angry and self-justify that you're the cause of the problem, the unilateral, punitive decision-maker hurting their career. In contrast, *guilt* is internal—as a human emotion, it forces people to look inward and see themselves more honestly and objectively by assuming partial responsibility for the problem at hand. And that's the ultimate way to resolve conduct and attitude problems in the workplace: by helping workers look internally and introspectively at whether they want to recommit to the organization or resign.

The value of this paid leave is that it forces the individual to engage in self-critical insight without the traditional trappings of formal progressive discipline. The worker won't walk away thinking, "I can't believe my boss gave me a final written warning and is docking my pay; she's a terrible manager." Rather, "Wow, I can't believe I'm getting a day off to consider whether I want to continue working here or to resign. I'm shocked that she'd accept my resignation and that she'd be supportive of my leaving the company. I guess I'd better be good, and although I don't like any of this, I respect how she's handling it and realize that I need to turn things around."

See the immediate paradigm shift in the employee's thought process? The value proposition of decision-making leaves is that they elevate employees in the process by empowering them to take control of the situation. And the hands-off nature of the exercise removes any semblance of judgment, replacing it with an objective, no-nonsense standard that the employee completely manages. In short, it's not about the company or the manager at all; it's strictly about the employee's willingness to reinvent herself in light of these issues being formally brought to her attention.

Even if this intervention doesn't work and the employee must be terminated nevertheless, using decision-making leaves is still beneficial. You'll demonstrate your reasonableness as a responsible organizational leader, and your company gains the advantage of creating a record that will minimize legal scrutiny should this ever turn into a wrongful termination case. You'll have shifted the paradigm away from "irresponsible company did little to proactively rehabilitate a good worker with temporary performance problems" to "responsible corporate citizen went out of its way to help proactively rehabilitate a worker and communicate the severity of the problem as well as future expectations, but employee refused to respond responsibly." Either way—as a thoughtful and caring frontline leader or as a legally sensitive organization trying to minimize potential liability—the company wins.

This decision-making leave strategy is a low-profile, low-drama type of employee intervention strategy that speaks volumes in its subtlety. As a tool in your management toolbox, it may be just the fix necessary to help others see things your way, keep them out of harm's way, and protect your company all at the same time.

Finally, decision-making leaves are generally rare and should be used only in situations when warranted (as in our three examples listed above). Also, never use them in cases when excessive absenteeism is the problem: the last thing the worker needs is more time off! Further, the goal is *not* to make a decision-making leave part of your regular corrective action process in which, for example, no one gets terminated without a decision-making leave first. Used on a situation-specific, case-by-case basis, however, this tool can do wonders for turning around employees with attitude problems or otherwise protecting your company from the legal liability associated with terminating long-term workers.

# LAST-CHANCE AGREEMENTS IN CONJUNCTION WITH FINAL WRITTEN WARNINGS

T he final written warning is a last-chance agreement between employer and employee regarding sustainable, improved performance or conduct. A breached final written warning normally should result in discharge; otherwise, you sabotage the integrity of your entire discipline system.

Whereas written warnings provide one more chance should a further infraction occur, final written warnings offer fewer alternatives. As a result, here's the typical language for a final written warning:

> This is your last chance, and your position is now in immediate jeopardy of being lost. Failure to demonstrate immediate and sustained improvement will result in further disciplinary action, up to and including dismissal.

Nevertheless, if the employee breaches the terms of a final written warning, but you don't feel that you're on solid legal ground to terminate, you may have to give the employee another chance. This typically occurs when the final incident is not clear and convincing or when the employee has so much tenure with the company that providing him with another chance is reasonable.

For example, suppose you have a male manager who has been accused of making sexual innuendos and creating a hostile work environment, but you found that certain witnesses agreed with the manager that no harassment occurred. In fact, some of these witnesses attest that the female employee not only engaged in but also initiated sexually oriented jokes and comments. If the manager has already received a final written warning for violating your company's sexual harassment policy, could you opt to terminate him based on this investigation? Possibly not, since the conflicting and contradictory testimony from those witnesses muddies the waters. Without a clean final incident, it might be difficult to justify termination. Still, the manager shouldn't have engaged in or allowed such discussions in the workplace, so discipline is certainly appropriate. Therefore, you might opt to state the following in the new disciplinary notice to the manager:

On [date], you received a final written notice stating that should you ever again engage in conduct that violates our company's sexual harassment policy, you could face further disciplinary action, up to and including dismissal. Our recent investigation reveals that you may have engaged in and allowed conversations that could have potentially created an unfriendly work environment. But because there is no agreement as to who began or encouraged the conversations that occurred on [date], we are not terminating you at this time. We are, instead, giving you another chance.

Be advised that this is your last chance. No future transgressions of this critical company policy will be permitted under any circumstances. You will be held responsible for any such complaints that arise under your purview, and immediate termination may result.

In addition, I remind you that our company has zero tolerance for violations of its antidiscrimination and harassment policies. Furthermore, no form of retaliation will be allowed against those employees who come forward to human resources with a good faith complaint.

In taking this action against the manager, you would neither violate the terms and conditions of the final warning nor set a dangerous precedent. Instead, you would fit the discipline to the offense, protect the employees who made the original complaint, and accord the manager due process. You would also avoid a wrongful discharge claim stemming from controversial witness statements— just the type of confusion and inconsistency that plaintiffs' attorneys love. Also, in this case, it would be appropriate to discipline the female employee for engaging in or instigating inappropriate conversations with the male manager.

Note: a final written warning is a *last-step option*. Different companies use different last-step options, and which one they use depends on their culture, history, and philosophy of discipline. Following are the five most common forms of last-step options, along with my recommendations concerning their use:

1. *Final Written Warning.* Recommended. The benefit of using this term is that it's clear and logically follows the verbal and written disciplinary actions that precede it.
2. *Probation.* Acceptable. Some companies prefer not to use the term *final written warning* and instead imply it by stating: "If you fail to follow established departmental policies and procedures at any time in the next ninety days, you will be placed on a *formal ninety-day probation*. If you fail to follow procedures or meet minimum performance standards in that

probationary period, you will be dismissed." That formal ninety-day probation is actually equivalent to the final written warning.

3. *Last-Chance Agreement.* Recommended. Some companies, however, use last-chance agreements as separate, freestanding documents. I recommend including last-chance agreement language in the disciplinary document itself. Therefore, we won't use last-chance agreements *as* the final step of discipline but *in* the final steps of discipline.

4. *Unpaid Suspension.* Not generally recommended because of the punitive nature of the punishment. By withholding an hourly employee's pay, there is a shaming element that forces the employee to explain the paycheck variance to family members, which is embarrassing. (Unpaid suspension should not be used with exempt workers due to wage and hour rules.) This harkens back to the dark days of industrial management when sticks were used to punish rather than carrots to motivate.

There are several serious disadvantages to using unpaid suspension. First, this action is negative, not affirmative. Therefore, it will likely fly in the face of your company's mission statement or belief about treating employees with dignity and respect. Second, unpaid suspension places an economic burden on the employee's family. In a sense, the family pays for the worker's performance and/or conduct problems, since pay is withheld. And third, placing an employee on unpaid suspension tends to create a martyr syndrome when employees share their woes with one another. The "bad" company takes advantage of the "helpless" employee by humiliating him in front of his family and causing him to lose face. Therefore, I recommend that you typically avoid traditional unpaid disciplinary suspensions whenever possible.

5. *Decision-Making Leave.* Highly recommended, if applicable. Organizations that want to achieve best practices in their employee relations activities place employees on one-day *paid* disciplinary leaves, also known as *decision-making leaves* or *days of contemplation.* In stark contrast to the historical and punitive suspension without pay, the decision-making leave removes the "defacing" mechanism from the discipline process and helps employees focus on their behaviors rather than on yours. However, while these actions tend to work very effectively, they're typically only used in certain circumstances, as outlined in chapter 18.

# 20

## HELD HOSTAGE BY UNDERPERFORMERS

### STRATEGIC GROUP TURNAROUNDS WHEN A TEAM IS ON THE BRINK OF FAILURE

The term *turnaround expert* typically refers to people who take a failing company and restore it to profitability—but it can also refer to a leader who develops a reputation for restoring a team of employees to success. The need for leadership turnaround experts is never higher than when a team or department appears to be on the brink of failure—when the entire functional area may be about to implode. As challenging as these situations may be, you'll rarely get an opportunity to effect change more than in situations in which struggling teams need immediate performance turnarounds. Your ability to restore your team to high performance will speak volumes about the value that you bring to your company.

When teams appear ready to implode, your first step should be to find out what may be driving a sudden change in employee behavior. Look for changes in circumstance: crises typically occur when organizations ratchet up performance expectations, adjust sales commission formulas downward, or introduce new technologies that appear to limit workers' discretion or freedom of choice. Workers sometimes resist change vehemently and demonstrate their dissatisfaction by engaging in work slowdowns, undermining one another, or colluding to entrap their boss.

Second, evaluate your frontline leadership team (typically, supervisors and leads). Strong leaders can typically take change in stride, keeping their teams focused on achieving results—even when the immediate change at hand may be unsettling or otherwise disruptive to daily busy operations. But when teams appear to be on the brink of failure, the immediate leaders are sometimes the core of the problem. Leaders who fail to provide an appropriate amount of communication, who demonstrate little respect for others, or who suffer from excessive drama and meltdowns in their areas may cause such problems or at least not be able to control problematic subordinates driving the dissatisfaction level on the team.

Third, look to those strong individual voices who exhibit a disproportionate influence over others at times like these. Departments in distress are often being overtaken by negative influencers who intimidate others and act as ringleaders of negativity—sometimes even intimidating their bosses, who avoid them at every turn. When leaders themselves drive such problems, handling matters appropriately takes on even more significance.

Let's take a look at a scenario in which you, the department head, discover a multitude of problems with one individual leader who continues to bully others. The way you handle such a quagmire is critical in terms of maintaining a healthy environment for the rest of the team and creating the proper written record to protect your department from legal scrutiny and premature turnover.

■ ■ ■

## CREATING AN APPROPRIATE
## WRITTEN RECORD FOR THE GROUP

"Professional plaintiffs" become very adept at keeping others at bay, and what works in their favor is that people tend to avoid them—and the conflict inherent in challenging them. So, they often act with impunity as if no one could touch them or otherwise hold them accountable. They often receive "meets expectations" performance review scores and no progressive discipline is initiated, as peers or subordinates refuse to speak out for fear of retaliation. So, on paper at least, their behavior is tolerated, and their personnel records indicate no particular problem or concern with their performance. In fact, these problematic performers and workplace bullies may be the first to invoke the services of a lawyer, claiming that they themselves are being bullied and are the victim of a system run amok.

Here's what the plaintiff's attorney's argument typically sounds like: "Her manager avoids her, and the company is clearly cutting a wide swath around her, withholding key responsibilities from her and otherwise not giving her a chance to excel in her role." Then comes the claim that this is all occurring because her supervisor harbors some animus against her because of her protected status (such as age, race, gender, or the like). This is the perfect formula for a discrimination claim from someone who's a lackluster performer with a negative attitude who's actually the cause—not the recipient—of the problematic conduct that's undermining the workplace.

The written record can change, however, only if you work with HR or your department head to investigate the team's allegations. Assuming everyone seems to get along fine with one another except for this one individual leader who aggressively confronts anyone who might challenge her, then you have an excellent opportunity to hold a group meeting and share perceptions of what you've learned and also reset management's expectations.

Depending on what you learn during your investigational meetings, you then have the opportunity to issue letters of clarification to recap management's expectations for all members of the team. (See chapter 17 for more information on letters of clarification.) With everyone starting with a fresh beginning, you can literally rewelcome everyone to the company and notify them that we all have an opportunity to start afresh. With the appropriate written record in place outlining future expectations, you'll be providing all individuals involved with an opportunity to reinvent themselves in light of management's new prerogatives. You'll have created a line in the sand that clarifies any confusion and that allows the wound to heal. Any future transgressions should be reported directly to you, and you've now provided a simple solution that invites everyone on the team back to normalcy.

## RESETTING MANAGEMENT'S EXPECTATIONS FOR THE PROBLEMATIC LEADER

Besides reestablishing group expectations, you also have the opportunity to follow up with the individual leader whom you find to be at the heart of the problem. Depending on what you learn during the investigation and group mediation, this individual may receive formal corrective action (in this case, a written or final written warning) in addition to the group letter of clarification. Suitability for the leadership role should also be explored and discussed with the individual.

With a written record in place that addresses both group expectations and the individual's specific workplace conduct issues, you'll have furnished sufficient documentation to restore order to the team. The leader will have been notified in writing about the company's concerns, thereby according her workplace due process in the form of documented corrective action.

Management can now take back control and mitigate this employee's negative influence on the rest of the team. Thus, if she ultimately files a lawsuit, you will have a record that is written on your terms, not hers. At her next performance review, it should be noted that she does not meet minimum expectations for the entire review year due to this significant final written warning. This way, you'll have a final written warning on record, combined with a failed annual performance review, in addition to no merit increase or bonus. That's the kind of record you need to deal with this type of caustic behavior and remove it from your workplace.

The team can then begin to heal and regain its self-confidence. Once these workplace bullies have been called out and their cases are appropriately documented, they typically resign quietly within a few months, because they miss the self-imposed drama; they realize they've cut off their future prospects within the organization; and they perceive that they have been diminished in the eyes of their coworkers—the very people they chose to bully and intimidate. They leave without filing a lawsuit because that avenue will have been cut off for them via the paper trail that is now in place. And so, the workplace is reinvigorated and set right again to return to productivity and peace of mind.

## A MODEL PAPER TRAIL

Progressive discipline has many practical uses, but one of its key strengths lies in breaking the chain of positive performance reviews on file. Assuming that a four-year employee has three years of acceptable reviews and will soon receive a fourth annual review, the progressive discipline might influence the written record as follows:

YEAR 1
No progressive discipline on file
Annual Performance Review *"Meets Expectations"*

YEAR 2
No progressive discipline on file
Annual Performance Review *"Meets Expectations"*

YEAR 3
No progressive discipline on file
Annual Performance Review *"Meets Expectations"*

YEAR 4
February: Documented verbal warning issued
May: Written warning issued
September: Final written warning issued
December: Annual Performance Review *"Fails to Meet Expectations"*

Should a clean final incident occur that violates the terms of the final written warning, the termination decision will be clear and defensible. The annual review captures the errant behavior or subpar performance, and the record is consistent in justifying the termination.

## A PROBLEMATIC PAPER TRAIL

Unfortunately, too many employers find themselves at a disadvantage if they issue corrective action but then fail to capture it during the annual performance review. Let's look at year 4 again with this all-too-common problematic record in place:

YEAR 4
February: Documented verbal warning issued
May: Written warning issued
September: Final written warning issued
December: Annual Performance Review "*Meets Expectations*"

Should a clean final incident occur that violates the terms of the final written warning, the termination decision becomes muddled because of the inconsistency in the record you've inadvertently created. In essence, despite the verbal, written, and final written warnings that were issued, you gave the employee the message that the performance for that entire year was "acceptable" and "met expectations." This is why grade inflation on the annual performance review remains such a problem for so many organizations. Remember, consistency in the record must extend from the progressive discipline to the annual performance review. The annual review captures what happened that year, and to paper over the disciplinary history by inflating the annual performance appraisal score could limit your ability to terminate when the time comes. In essence, the inflated annual review could place a massive roadblock in your way in terms of terminating for a clean violation of the final written warning.

# PART 3

# TERMINATIONS FOR CAUSE, LAYOFFS, AND NEGOTIATED RESIGNATIONS

This section describes how to handle various situations that often arise when you need to terminate one or more employees. Terminations, unfortunately, are a reality in any business, but you want to ensure that employees are separated professionally and in a legally defensible way.

With that in mind, this section discusses the importance of considering all factors pertaining to an employee and his or her performance *before* you terminate (to maintain morale for the survivors and prevent potential lawsuits). It describes when and how to offer a separation package instead of terminating an employee if that situation seems appropriate. It covers what you need to know about laying off employees instead of terminating them for cause and how to handle summary discharges and requests for "resignations by mutual consent" (instead of a termination for cause). Knowing how to deal with all these situations will help ensure that you—and your company—are dealing fairly with employees so that you won't have further (legal) problems down the line.

# 21

# VETTING THE RECORD
# BEFORE RECOMMENDING TERMINATION

Terminating an employee is necessary occasionally. Before doing so, make sure that you're accounting for the key issues that any plaintiff's attorney will consider in evaluating a case and determining whether to bring suit against your organization. You'll also want to be doubly sure you're not missing anything that can be material to the final decision-making process. In terms of the individual being considered for termination, review the following before recommending any termination action. However, use it only as a reference checklist; do not fill it in and place it in an employee's personal file or investigation folder, as it may be subject to legal discovery.

## TERMINATION CHECKLIST (FOR REVIEW ONLY)
### DO NOT FILL OUT OR PLACE IN AN EMPLOYEE'S FILE

Please review the following elements when preparing to recommend an employee termination. Share any relevant issues with senior management and/or legal counsel during pre-termination discussions.

Date of hire: _____

Length of tenure: _____

Age (there are key protections for employees ages forty and above):

_____

Ethnicity: _____

Gender: _____

Corrective action history: _____

_____

_____

_____

_____

Most recent performance review score and overall performance review history: _____

_____

_____

_____

_____

Length of time in current position: _____

Prior positions held within our company: _____

Open workers' compensation claim(s):

Yes ☐   No ☐

Open intermittent Family and Medical Leave Act (FMLA) claim(s):

Yes ☐   No ☐

Disability status: For example, is the company currently engaging in the Americans with Disabilities Act (ADA) "interactive process" with this individual or otherwise granting some form of protected leave, modified duty, or other reasonable accommodation?

Yes ☐   No ☐

Pregnancy status:

Yes ☐   No ☐

Possibility of a retaliation charge for having lodged a good faith complaint against the organization ("whistleblower" protection): Yes ☐ No ☐

Supervisor's age, ethnicity, and gender (to counter any potential claims of discrimination): _____

How long the supervisor has managed this employee: _____

Whether the supervisor originally hired the employee. (If so, a discrimination claim may be more difficult to prove): Yes ☐ No ☐

Specifics regarding the final/most recent incident that could justify termination: _____

_____

_____

_____

_____

Did we learn the employee's side of the story at this point? Yes ☐ No ☐

Any mitigating circumstances regarding the final incident: Yes ☐ No ☐

If so, explain: _____

_____

_____

_____

Other factors: _____

_____

_____

_____

Armed with this short list of guidelines to practical workplace investigations, you can then objectively determine whether a "clean final incident" justifies a termination for cause. The nature of the final incident that triggers termination is exceptionally important. The more specific and concrete the violation, the stronger the justification to terminate. For example, if the newest incident clearly violates the terms of a final written warning, you should be safe to terminate. Similarly, if the incident stems from some form of egregious misconduct such as theft, embezzlement, or fraud, you should likewise be safe to terminate as a "summary offense" (meaning that no prior corrective action is warranted because the one-time occurrence justifies outright dismissal).

In comparison, avoid minimal final incidents that could appear insubstantial or otherwise appear to lack objectivity. For example, if the record you're relying on to justify a termination appears as if you were looking for a reason to fire the person, then your credibility could be challenged. So could the validity of your decision to terminate the individual.

The best yardstick: Ask yourself, "If one of our best employees engaged in a similar infraction, would discipline be warranted?" If the answer is no, then the final incident may not be substantial enough to warrant dismissal. But if the answer is yes, you can feel more confident that you're being consistent in the application of your own rules and that the termination decision will withstand legal scrutiny.

When in doubt, check with qualified legal counsel. With HR's or your attorney's review and approval, you'll be much better prepared to address exceptional situations not only with the confidence that comes from knowledge but also with the wisdom that comes from experience.

# 22

# NEGOTIATING SEPARATION PACKAGES WHEN NO PROGRESSIVE DISCIPLINE IS ON FILE

P art 2 covered how to implement progressive discipline to ensure that your company follows due process with your employees. But you may find yourself in a situation in which you want to separate an employee who has not been granted progressive discipline. How do you go about terminating someone whose presence poses a problem but who has no progressive disciplinary actions or unacceptable performance evaluations on file? This is a tough question.

You may have the right to terminate employees at will. Even so, if you're challenged, you will have to prove that you followed your organization's policies and past practices in arriving at that decision. If your defense isn't adequate and the employee's attorney can prove that the employment relationship was indeed not at will and that termination required good-cause justification, then you will most likely have to settle out of court.

When you are faced with this predicament, consider meeting with the employee and explaining the situation openly. If you are fair with the person and allow for a transitional period, then you will likely increase your chances for an amicable parting. Perks that you can offer to entice an employee to agree to a "separation by mutual consent" (discussed later in this section) or a "negotiated termination" include:

- Separation packages: separation payouts should be awarded only after signed releases have been obtained. The separation money is the legal consideration in exchange for the release. And remember that the Older Workers Benefit Protection Act (OWBPA), which amended the Age Discrimination in Employment Act (ADEA) of 1967, mandates that workers over age forty be given a minimum of twenty-one days of notice and an additional seven days in which to rescind the agreement.
- Outplacement (career transition) services.
- Uncontested unemployment benefits.
- A neutral letter of recommendation strictly based on historical performance evaluation feedback: be wary of stilted letters of recommendation that portray only positive attributes. You have a moral and legal obligation to provide both positive and negative information in the assessment. In addition, you're obliged to provide truthful, objective information in good faith and without malice to a prospective employer who requests the information and has a need to know. If the material you provide the prospective employer is false or misrepresentative and the company relies on your recommendation and hires the individual, you could be named in a negligent-hiring lawsuit further down the road if that employee later becomes violent, sexually harasses another person, or commits a similar substantial breach of conduct (assuming that you're separating the employee for one of those reasons). On the other hand, the employee can sue you for defamation if your characterization in the letter

appears biased. It's not hard to see why providing references on past employees is a catch-22, no-win situation for most employers.

Hopefully, your cooperation in focusing the individual on a future career in a different company will be viewed as realistic and fair. That path of least resistance may give the worker an easy way out that simultaneously allows her to save face. And once again, you'll maintain a workplace that fosters respect, dignity, fairness, and open communications.

On the other hand, be sure to let the employee know this will be her choice and that you'll respect whatever decision she makes. (After all, you're paying now for some other supervisor's failure to document performance problems clearly both in annual performance reviews and written warnings.) For example, you might say:

Ava, I'm guessing that you're not totally happy with our working relationship, and truth be told, I'm not either. I've discussed this with our division head and also with human resources, and I've asked Olivia from human resources to join us in this meeting so that we could discuss some options.

In fairness, I want you to know that I told Olivia that I need to begin the progressive discipline process and draft a written warning for you based on the events that occurred yesterday. Still, I feel like there's a bigger issue at hand, so to start initiating progressive disciplinary measures that could lead to your termination may not do either of us much good.

Olivia thought it might be better for us to sit down with you and lay our cards on the table. In short, if you're not happy in this role and want to avoid blemishing your record with written warnings and substandard performance reviews that could ultimately lead to a termination for cause, maybe we could work out some terms that will allow you to remain in control of the situation and walk out with your head held high.

I've gotten approval to offer you a three-month separation package that will allow you to continue paying for your medical benefits at your current rate. If you choose to accept that package, you'd need to sign a release absolving the company from liability. And you don't have to answer us now: you could think about this and let us know later this week if it's an option you'd like to pursue.

I don't want to discount the years you've worked for us, Ava. Also, if it were me in this situation, I would prefer that my boss had enough respect for me to tell me openly and honestly that it might be better for me to pursue different teams in other leagues.

If you choose to accept the package, we won't contest your un-employment. You can tell everyone on the team that you're leaving for whatever reason you deem fit, and of course when you apply at other companies and fill in that "Reason for Leaving" line on the employment application, you could show that you left us rather than vice versa.

If you choose not to take this offer, that's fine, too. At that point, though, I'll ask Olivia to help me draft the written warning that we were going to prepare before we started this meeting today. I'll also ask her help in discussing with us both how I can provide you with additional support. Again, I'll respect whatever decision you make. Just let me know in the next few days how you're feeling about all of this, okay?

It's important that you have a third-party witness (in this case, human resources) at a meeting like this; otherwise, the employee could argue that you forced her to quit by threatening termination if she didn't. That could lead to a "constructive discharge" claim where the worker claims she felt compelled to quit because of intolerable working conditions and which looks for similar remedies under the law as a wrongful discharge claim. If it's just one person's word against another's, it may make it difficult for you, the employer, to defend yourself against the employee's allegations.

For the same reason, it's important that the employee realize that if she doesn't agree to accept the separation package, she'll receive a written warning. Ava needs to know that up front before she makes her decision. Otherwise, it will appear as if you're giving her a warning after she decides not to resign, and in a judge's or arbitrator's eyes, that could easily appear to be retaliatory behavior on your part. It goes without saying that your strategy session with human resources or outside counsel in a situation like this is critical *before* you engage in any conversations with the employee.

Finally, your offer doesn't have to include a separation package in exchange for a release. Instead, you may simply opt to allow the employee to look for another full-time job while employed with your firm:

Ava, I'm guessing that you're not totally happy with our working relationship, and truth be told, neither am I. I've discussed this with our division head and also with human resources, and I've asked Olivia from human resources to join us in this meeting so that we could discuss some options.

If you'd like to pursue looking for a full-time position elsewhere, I could support that. I'd rather we be honest and up front with one another right from the start so that you don't have to feel like you have to walk on eggshells or make up an excuse every time you land an interview.

If you'd like to pursue this option, though, please keep two things in mind: First, we still come first. You'd need to give me twenty-four hours' advance notice whenever you'd have an inter-view planned so that we could divvy up the workload and reassign responsibilities as appropriate. Second, it's time that we put our con-cerns down in writing in the form of a formal written warning. This has been necessary for quite some time now, and your choosing to launch a job search, if that's indeed what you choose to do, really can't get in the way of the written record that we need to create.

For now, we'll prepare the written warning draft. Please give some thought to the option of initiating a job search, and I'll be as flexible for you as I can. What are your thoughts about that?

The written warning at this point is important because Ava's willingness to launch a job search shouldn't hold you back from managing her performance and holding her to high expectations. Many unsuspecting employers have allowed individuals to begin interviews elsewhere, only later to find that they have taken advan-tage of the situation and not kept their word. If that's the case with Ava, then having that written warning on file now gives you a lot more leverage to move through the progressive discipline system a month or two from now if you learn that she's not keeping her end of the bargain by engaging in a serious job search.

In short, protect yourself and your company by placing a stake in the ground the day you hold this conversation so that you don't lose a few months in the progressive discipline process by having to start from scratch months later—after you realize that the em-ployee didn't uphold her end of the bargain.

# 23

# SUMMARY OFFENSES (IMMEDIATE DISCHARGE)

Terminations for first-time offenses are always challenging for managers. While most managers assume that written warnings are the norm before terminating someone, not all offenses in the workplace are subject to progressive discipline. If someone steals from your company, the organization has the right to terminate immediately, even for a first-time offense. In fact, failing to do so could make your company appear irresponsible and set a dangerous precedent in terms of your ability to terminate future thieves. After all, it doesn't make much sense to give someone a written warning after they steal cash from the register stating, "If you ever steal cash from the register again, you'll be terminated."

As you might guess, employers have a significant amount of discretion to move to summary (immediate) dismissal for *conduct*-related infractions like stealing, fraud, embezzlement, and gross insubordination. When it comes to *performance*- and *attendance*-related transgressions, employers are typically expected to go through all the normal steps of progressive discipline as accorded under company policy and practice.

This section addresses the tough conversations that are necessary when faced with cases of summary, or immediate, dismissal. In all cases, act reasonably and responsibly and avoid demonstrating contempt or "throwing them out on their ear." Let cooler heads prevail, even at times when you're exceptionally angry and disappointed. After all, treating people with respect and dignity at the finish line should be a core element of your culture—despite the sometimes crazy and irresponsible things that workers do from time to time.

Of course, you also have the right to look into pursuing the individual legally for post-termination reimbursement to the company, but that should be discussed with legal counsel. At that point, you'll need to determine whether any collection action on your part will be worth the expense of pursuing it and balancing that opportunity cost against the lesson you wish to give the perpetrator on principle.

Finally, note that "You're fired!" is not a nice way to end anyone's employment, as it deprives the person of respect. Although you may feel that the employee has forfeited any right to dignity by his egregious actions, keep in mind that firing people on the spot is best left for reality TV. When you suspect that a summary dismissal may be warranted, it's typically best to send the employee home with pay on an "administrative" or "investigatory" leave so that he is off the premises and you have the time to investigate the matter more thoroughly (for example, with your employment attorney).

Terminating the individual over the phone while he's at home can then take place, which provides you and your company with more safety while allowing feelings of anger and resentment to subside. Besides, you'll make a much better record for the company if you place the individual on paid administrative leave before rushing to judgment, and courts and juries favor that type of corporate wisdom and restraint. Of course, it's always preferable to terminate in person rather than over the phone, but exceptions may arise, especially when safety concerns are involved.

Let's take a look at five common scenarios that might lead to summary discharge: employee theft, time-card fraud, threats of violence in the workplace, sexual harassment, and insubordination.

## EMPLOYEE THEFT

Employee theft is a multibillion-dollar business, with estimates ranging from $20 to $50 billion per year in US companies. It comes in many forms: retail theft of clothing and apparel, funneling and diverting accounting funds away from the company and into a personal bank account, absconding with old computers that were meant for corporate donations, and even pilfering company charity donations and writing them off as if they were a personal donation for tax purposes.

Whatever the form, employee theft should be addressed swiftly and definitively. Of course, you'll always want to hear and document the employee's side of the story before initiating termination proceedings. Just remember that even if you've caught the misdeed on tape and have witnesses willing to sign statements of testimony, you absolutely want to listen to the employee's side of the story to ensure workplace due process. Strange things happen in the workplace, and sometimes what you see isn't necessarily "what is," especially if someone is being set up. For example, suppose you have video (from your surveillance monitoring system) of an employee putting equipment in his truck and driving off with it; before you accuse that employee of stealing, ask him if he can explain those actions: it's possible that someone else instructed him to remove that equipment, so be wary of jumping to conclusions.

## TIME-CARD FRAUD

This is a tough problem, because employees often don't realize it's not necessarily subject to steps of progressive discipline and can be interpreted as a summary offense. Depending on the nature of the incident, its severity, and the number of times it has occurred, a company has the discretion to terminate once the offense is discovered. It helps very much if the company has a timekeeping policy that states that violations are not subject to the progressive discipline process and may result in immediate discharge.

To be clear, not every incident of time-card misrepresentation must result in termination. For example, if an employee showed on her time-card that she worked until 5:00 p.m. one day last week but actually left the office at 4:30 p.m., that would probably be best addressed by a short discussion stating that you expect people to carefully log when they clock in and out and not simply fill in a "missed punch" the next day with the incorrect time. That's especially the case if this is a first occurrence. Certain infractions, however, should be interpreted as summary offenses—for example, if two employees continuously punch in for one another so the alternating employee can come in later without being docked time. Multiple falsifications of the actual hours worked will likely result in termination for both employees. Time is a proxy for money in the workplace.

## THREATS OF VIOLENCE IN THE WORKPLACE

Generally speaking, companies have little discretion in responding to threats of violence. That's because once the company is put on notice that one employee is threatening another, the company has an affirmative obligation to protect the threatened employee and provide for a safe and secure workplace for everyone else. Should the company not take the threat seriously and injury or death results, the company could find itself liable for a host of violations, including negligent hiring, negligent retention, negligent infliction of emotional distress, and other tort claims. Both direct and veiled threats may fall under this summary dismissal context, depending on the circumstances.

## SEXUAL HARASSMENT

Sexual harassment may be a summary offense, or it may be subject to progressive discipline: it depends on the nature of the individual's conduct, the egregiousness of the offense, and myriad other factors. One situation that requires summary termination is when an employee claims that she was "forced" to sleep with someone higher up the career ladder, because she felt if she didn't comply, she would face retaliation and ultimately dismissal. This is a typical case of quid pro quo harassment in which sexual favors effectively become a condition of employment.

It's not uncommon for the manager to defend himself by arguing that the relationship was consensual. The problem is that you'll be facing a he-said/she-said situation in which you (or a jury) can't know the truth, so the victim's allegations become the standard of judgment. In short, there's little defense that a company could proffer if one of its supervisors engages in sexual relationships with a subordinate. These cases pose unusually serious legal threats to your organization, so when you are faced with this type of claim, get immediate help from your human resources department in addition to qualified legal counsel.

## INSUBORDINATION

Insubordination is a conduct infraction that stems from one of two things: (1) intentionally disregarding a supervisor's explicit directive or (2) demonstrating extreme disrespect for a supervisor, either in private or in front of others. Insubordination may be subject either to progressive discipline or to summary discharge. A lot will depend on the circumstances surrounding the event, the employee's history with the company, and the egregiousness of the offense. Don't rush to judgment: if immediate termination is the ultimate result, it would be better to make it a quiet and low-key event with the employee waiting at home while on investigatory leave rather than a "shootout at the OK Corral"–style conflagration in front of the whole staff.

When an employee appears to blow up and spew expletives at a supervisor in front of the rest of the staff, your best bet as the supervisor will be to end the meeting, dismiss the rest of the staff, and ask the employee to meet with you in private in your office. If you have a human resources department on-site or available via phone or video, ask that a member of the HR team join you to moderate the meeting. After all, no matter how much you pride yourself on your objectivity and fairness in managing others, once you're a participant in the game, you can no longer play the role of referee and mediator. You'll need an objective third party to do that, and human resources or another member of the management team can join you as the arbiter of the dispute.

Finally, remember that no terminations should be made without human resources' and senior management's approval. No corporate leader has the discretion to terminate someone on the spot. To do so could risk your own job as well as personal financial liability (for acting outside the course and scope of your employment). No matter how high your level of frustration, no matter how clear the evidence appears to you, save the job of terminating the individual for someone else. You may be in the meeting at the time the termination is communicated, but there's far too much risk these days in making unilateral termination decisions without input and approval from senior management and HR.

**24**

# TERMINATIONS FOR CAUSE
# VERSUS RESIGNATIONS BY MUTUAL CONSENT

Sometimes, a manager is asked to allow someone to "resign by mutual consent" rather than be terminated for cause. While your natural instinct may be to allow the individual to resign on his own terms, think carefully about this option before granting it.

Generally speaking, any ambiguity in the termination process could be held against your organization. If an employee fails to abide by the terms of a final written warning or exhibits egregious misconduct, for example, then termination is appropriate. Lessening the blow by allowing the employee to resign or placing the individual on an inactive status while keeping him on the payroll while he conducts a job search could be interpreted as signs of weakness on the part of the employer, or worse, as a tacit acknowledgment that the company was partly at fault for the situation. This falls under the heading of "no good deed goes unpunished," so be hesitant about granting employees the right to resign when all the termination paperwork and processing is in place. Such last-minute negotiation attempts from an employee who is about to be terminated blur the record you've created. Simply follow through with the termination as planned. If the employee is worried about having a termination on record as far as references go, simply confirm that your company only shares dates of employment plus last title held when it comes to references and employment verifications: no details regarding the employee's reason for leaving the organization will be shared.

It is important to avoid sugarcoating terminations. Assuming you've accorded the employee workplace due process in the form of progressive discipline, follow your company's policies and practices, and avoid exceptions. That's especially true in cases of "summary dismissals" (that is, immediate terminations without prior corrective action) for egregious misconduct, such as theft, forgery, fraud, record falsification, workplace violence, or severe cases of harassment or bullying. Allowing someone to resign in order to "save face" may feel less punitive, but it lays out a record in which the organization did not terminate for an immediately terminable offense, which could create an unwanted precedent in your employment practices. The bottom line is that any ambiguity in the termination record that you create can and will be used against your company in the litigation arena.

Terminations for cause should be a straightforward management practice. Your good intentions may be distorted if a former employee tries to avert blame and may be capitalized on if a plaintiff's attorney seeks to attribute ulterior motives to your benevolent actions. "After all," the reasoning may go, "why would the company allow him to resign if what he did was so egregious? It sounds like the company was trying to sweep something under the rug because of its own mishandling of the matter." When in doubt, always check with qualified legal counsel before agreeing to convert terminations for cause into employee resignations. Such allowances have come back to bite employers big-time, and the written record you create will always serve as your primary defense during litigation, so don't back off at the finish line.

## SPECIAL NOTE: PROVIDE EXITING EMPLOYEES WITH COPIES OF THEIR HISTORICAL PERFORMANCE REVIEWS

When you terminate someone, it may be a good practice to provide them with copies of their historical performance appraisals. They are then at liberty to share those reviews—if they choose to—with prospective employers as evidence of their performance in lieu of reference telephone calls or online questionnaires with prior supervisors. Simply tell the exiting employee, "We don't provide references to potential employers as a matter of policy, but you're free to share these historical annual reviews as proof of your performance levels. That should be enough for most employers and will allow them to check the 'References Completed' box on their new hire checklist—they simply want proof of your real-time performance, and performance reviews clearly document strengths, areas for development, and the like."

And voilà—no more guilt! Neither the prior manager nor human resources needs to feel bad for not helping the individual find a new position: the performance reviews speak for themselves, so take yourself out of the middle when it comes to guilt associated with not permitting someone to resign who should otherwise be terminated or for not providing references to prospective employers. Prior performance reviews take you out of the middle and place employees squarely responsible for their own career management and future employment opportunities.

# 25

# CAN AN EMPLOYEE
# RESCIND A VERBAL RESIGNATION?

What should you do when an employee—especially a poor performing and problematic one—gives notice and then changes her mind on the last day? Does she have a right to insist that you tear up her resignation letter or otherwise retain her before her two-week notice period runs out?

It depends. You have the right, as an employer, to rely on the individual's resignation in good faith and end her employment on the agreed-upon date. But as most employment lawyers will caution you, how you *act in reliance* on the notice becomes a key issue if the matter were to be pursued legally. Specifically, if you haven't truly "taken action in reliance" upon her resignation by posting her job, reassigning her work duties, and interviewing candidates, for example, then the employee may very well be free to rescind her resignation during the notice period in the eyes of a judge or arbitrator. In fact, if you could ideally fill the position within that two-week notice period by promoting someone internally or extending an offer to an external candidate, you would be on the strongest grounds to deny the employee's request to remain employed.

Further, there are a few commonsense steps you can take when an employee notifies you verbally that she is planning on leaving the company "in a few weeks" or "next month" or something other than with a firm date:

- Ask her to put her notice in writing with a firm date. Simply state that this is a company requirement so that you can plan ahead in terms of staffing and budget approvals.

- If the employee delays putting it in writing, simply email her a confirmation. The email codifies her verbal message so that a firm record is in place. A note to the individual could be drafted like: "Keisha, I appreciate your letting me know that you intend to resign your position on Friday, October 11. I will notify human resources of the change so they can obtain budget approval and post the position. I'm happy for you in your decision to relocate back to Chicago and wish you well with your move."

- If the employee says she's decided to leave the organization "three months from now" and without a firm date, that's tricky and you'll need help. First, if you have an HR department, reach out there initially. If there's no HR resource available, partner with your immediate boss and inform your department head and in-house counsel. Generic "three-month notices" don't count in terms of providing you with the information you need to prepare for the transition. Note that such employee notices often occur when employees are about to be written up, issued a final written warning, or placed on a performance improvement plan. They hope that you'll simply forget to issue the disciplinary warning since they've announced they're leaving. And surprise, surprise: three months from now they don't leave because their plans have changed. And you'll have missed that window three months earlier to discipline the individual. That's a bit of a sucker punch, and employers need to avoid that under all circumstances. You likewise have the right under most circumstances to inform the employee that two weeks' notice are all that's required and let the individual go at that point, but again, such circumstances can be problematic, so strategizing with qualified legal counsel is recommended.

The lesson? When a problematic and underperforming employee tenders notice, don't do a happy dance just yet: you still have work do. Specifically, fill the position as quickly as possible, or at least demonstrate that you acted in good faith in reliance on her resignation notice by posting the job, redistributing her work, and beginning both internal and external interviews. You'll have a much greater chance of warding off a wrongful termination claim if you can show that you acted on her notice rather than simply accepting the resignation letter and filing it away. Matters that may appear trivial or rote in the employment world can sometimes take on a new life under the scrutiny of a plaintiff attorney's microscope, so remember the adage *Forewarned is forearmed*: if you know about something before it happens, you can prepare better for it. Handling employee resignations properly isn't always as simple as you might think and can trigger a land mine if not managed proactively.

## LEADERSHIP TIP: MAKING THE RESIGNATION NOTICE DATE THE EMPLOYEE'S LAST DAY

If an employee provides two weeks' notice and you would prefer that the individual leave immediately on the day of notice, be sure to pay out the two-week notice period. That completes the resignation commitment that the employee established. Failing to do so could inadvertently convert the individual's "resignation" to a "termination" in the eyes of the law. If you were to be challenged, you likely would not be able to demonstrate cause in a potential wrongful termination lawsuit. Therefore, avoid setting a different termination date than the employee originally proffered by paying through that termination date to avoid stepping on a land mine that could cause future legal challenges.

**26**

# IF WE CAN'T TERMINATE SOMEONE, CAN WE SIMPLY LAY THEM OFF?

One of the biggest mistaken assumptions in the workplace is that companies can simply lay off their weakest performers rather than proceed with progressive discipline. In almost all cases, progressive discipline is the method of choice when it comes to dealing with substandard performance issues. To simply make the person and problem magically go away rarely works. Here's what you need to know so you can avoid this potentially dangerous land mine.

Managers who want to avoid the confrontation associated with progressive discipline and termination often look to the path of least resistance—a no-fault layoff—because it appears to provide a quicker solution to ending employment. But there are certain legal and practical guidelines that you need to follow when considering a layoff. Specifically, you need to evaluate the appropriate employee to be laid off, how long you'll have to wait before refilling that position, and what could happen if you were legally challenged for having improperly laid someone off.

First, keep in mind that you eliminate *positions,* not people. In other words, your written records must reflect that a position is being eliminated because of a legitimate business need, and the individual who currently fills that position will now be affected because there's no longer a job to report to. If removing a problem performer is your goal, then eliminating that individual's job may be a big mistake. After all, you'll still need to get the work done.

Second, determining which employee should be separated once you've established a legitimate business reason to eliminate a position can be challenging. Remember, you can't arbitrarily select someone for a layoff simply because he is your weakest performer or because he happens to be sitting in the seat that's being eliminated. Instead, you must first identify the *least-qualified person in the department or unit to assume the remaining duties.* The least-qualified person on paper, however, may end up being your best (albeit newest) performer.

Let's look at an example to clarify these concepts. Let's say you're looking to eliminate one of three administrative assistant positions in your marketing department. Since there are three individuals who currently fill the role of administrative assistant in marketing, you now have a pool to choose from, and your company will be required to conduct a "peer group analysis" to see which of the three current individuals is the least qualified to assume the remaining job responsibilities once the position is eliminated.

Initially, you'll want to develop a list of all employees in that group with similar titles and responsibilities. Second, review the nature of the remaining work to be done after the position is eliminated. For example, if the assistant position reporting to the digital/social media team is being considered for elimination, then document the responsibilities that will remain in the unit after the reduction in force. (Job descriptions are immensely helpful for such comparisons.)

Third, determine which of the three assistants in marketing is the least qualified to assume those remaining duties. In essence, you'll be comparing all three employees' essential job responsibilities, prior experience, skills, knowledge, abilities, education, and professional certifications. In addition, review the employees' annual performance reviews, tenure, and history of progressive discipline to create the appropriate written record. It would also make sense to review their work experience before joining your organization so that tenure alone doesn't outweigh other considerations.

Finally, once that documented comparison occurs for the three employees who could potentially qualify to perform the remaining work, then it's time to determine who is the least-qualified individual. If that individual is the person you originally targeted for the layoff because of his ongoing performance or conduct problems, then you may be safe to separate his employment.

But it's rare that it works out that way. It's more often the case that the underperforming employee is arguably not the least-qualified individual (based on your review of all relevant criteria). In fact, in my experience, the underperforming worker you'd like to lay off typically has the most tenure, coupled with a long history of performance reviews that "meet expectations." Under such circumstances, it could be exceptionally risky to select that individual for layoff (should a plaintiff's attorney later challenge your conclusion). Since your records don't support separating the problematic employee in question, then you'd have to lay off one of the other two assistants. Of course, that would mean that a layoff would no longer be a viable alternative for you since you can't use it to separate the one administrative assistant who's causing all the problems. Therefore, you'd have to revert to managing that individual's performance via documented progressive discipline.

But wait. There is another key consideration when determining if a layoff is the appropriate employer action when dealing with underperforming employees. You also need to keep in mind that courts and juries have certain expectations about employers' responsibilities when eliminating positions and laying off workers. The logic is simply this: if a company has a legitimate business reason to eliminate a position, then it probably shouldn't have a need to re-create that position in the near future. If the company were to do that, it could appear to a judge or jury that the company's original action was pretext. In other words, the court could be persuaded that the so-called "layoff" was really a termination for cause in disguise. This could obviously damage the company's credibility during litigation.

How long does the position need to remain unfilled? That depends on your state. In California, for example, there is a two-year statute of limitations on many unlawful employment practices if there was a potential violation of public policy. In other words, an ex-employee may file a complaint up to two years from the date that the unlawful practice occurred. So, California employers are safest waiting at least twenty-four months before filling a position that was previously eliminated.

What if this California employer were willing to gamble and fill the position after, say, twelve months? Well, if the ex-employee learned that his previous position was filled and he then engaged the services of a plaintiff's attorney to pursue the matter, then the damages sought would be similar to a wrongful termination claim. If you were held to a for-cause standard of termination, you could be burdened with providing documentation to show that you had reason to terminate the employee because of substandard job performance, inappropriate workplace conduct, or excessive absenteeism. And that's not an easy threshold to meet if you laid off someone who had no corrective action on file and was simply just the weakest performer in the selection pool in your opinion.

As a result, your company and the employee would probably need to reach an out-of-court settlement. Damages could include reimbursement for lost wages, compensation for emotional distress, plaintiff attorneys' fees, and, in egregious cases of employer misconduct, punitive damages. Here's the bottom line: progressive discipline is the optimal way to deal with substandard job performance or inappropriate workplace behavior. Trying to hide behind a layoff may feel easier to implement on the front end but could leave your company high and dry should the matter ultimately proceed to litigation.

# 27

# HEALING THE TEAM AFTER A TERMINATION OR DOWNSIZING

Coworker separations—because of resignations but especially due to layoffs or terminations—can make the remaining employees feel anxious, unnerved, and distressed. Restoring workplace confidence can be exceptionally challenging. How do you communicate difficult news so that your team members can heal the wound left by the departing employee(s)? The way you tell your employees about such a departure will vary slightly depending on the reason for the termination—that is, whether the separation is because of performance or attendance problems, due to misconduct, or because of layoffs.

In the first case, terminations for performance or attendance problems typically don't occur in a vacuum. Employees receive corrective action notices that convey that their job may be in jeopardy, and it's not uncommon for workers to share this with their peers in frustration and disappointment, either at themselves or at their boss. The cases where progressive discipline leads to termination for cause are typically not a surprise because the person's coworkers are often aware of the situation.

In fairly straightforward situations like these, it's okay to make a general statement to the team that John Doe is no longer with the company. The key is to keep it simple, respectful, and short. A straightforward announcement might sound something like this:

Everyone, I just wanted to call a meeting to let you know that John Doe is no longer with the company. John was with us for the past two and a half years, and we appreciate all his efforts over that time. But his separation became effective yesterday, and we'll discuss filling his position and temporarily reassigning some of his responsibilities to keep things moving along.

If you have any questions, please see me privately. Out of respect for John's privacy, I'd ask you all to please keep this confidential so we can ensure a smooth transition for everyone involved. Remember as well that any requests for employment references from outside parties like other employers or staffing firms must be referred to human resources. Thank you all.

Notice that the reason for the employee's departure isn't given for the sake of the individual's privacy as well as to demonstrate respect. This is fair, transparent, and above board, and that's a nice way of allowing the team members to heal and get on with their business.

If an employee has been terminated for egregious misconduct, this would have occurred because of such infractions as harassment, bullying, discrimination, violence, gross insubordination, theft, fraud, embezzlement, falsification of records, substance abuse, or the like. In these cases, the resulting termination can be more shocking because people don't know any details, and they might make incorrect assumptions. Therefore, the announcement, while similar to the previous example, should focus more on instructions and guidelines than simply providing notice of the person's departure. For example:

> Everyone, I called this meeting to let you know that Olivia Brown is no longer with the company. I'm not at liberty to discuss specifics with you, and out of respect for Olivia's privacy, I'll ask you not to engage in speculation regarding her leaving the company. I want you to know that we treated Olivia very respectfully, we listened carefully to what she had to say, and we took appropriate action based on our findings.
>
> What I'd specifically ask you to do is to refer all calls for references regarding Olivia's performance to HR. I'll remind you that we have a policy and active practice of not sharing references with outside third parties like prospective employers or headhunters, and violating that policy in this case could have grave consequences for both you and for the company.
>
> Further, out of respect for Olivia's privacy, I'm formally instructing you all to avoid any gossip or banter about Olivia or her separation from the company. Do I have your commitment?

Although such a message may appear to be shrouded in mystery, it's important that you remind everyone on your team not to engage in third-party reference checks under any circumstances. Doing so could open your organization to claims of breach of privacy and defamation (slander) and potentially hold the referent as well as your company liable for damages relating to lost wages due to a rescinded job offer. In other words, defamation claims have teeth, and no one on your team will want to see their names listed in a lawsuit that the departing employee filed against the organization and specific individuals within the company because a poor reference killed Olivia's chances of landing a new job.

Finally, layoffs are different from terminations for cause. In a termination, individuals are separated from the company for something that was under their control: failure to meet quality standards, to arrive on time, or to reach certain productivity thresholds, for example, that others are able to accomplish. In contrast, during layoffs, positions are eliminated and the people filling those positions are let go (often due to no fault of their own).

After an individual member of your team is laid off due to a position elimination, meet with the remaining members of your team to openly address and acknowledge what's occurred:

Everyone, I called this meeting to let you know that we've unfortunately had a position elimination in our department, and Jacob Smith has been laid off. I know it's always unnerving to hear these kinds of things, which is why I wanted to bring us all together to discuss this.

First, I want you to know that Jacob handled the news very professionally and said he'd be okay. He understands that he can be rehired in the future because he left the company in good standing. We've treated him with respect and dignity, and he responded in kind, so we're all on good terms. Therefore, there's no need to feel uncomfortable if you should see him outside of work.

Finally, we have no further plans of laying off anyone else after today. As a next step, we'll all take a close look at Jacob's responsibilities, as they'll need to be divided up among the rest of us. As always, I appreciate your support.

This is a respectable and professional way of handling communications about individual position eliminations because it answers the immediate questions that people have: "Will Jacob be well taken care of? Are our jobs in jeopardy now as well?" In short, answer the group's questions honestly and openly but refocus them on what's important—that they're all still employed and have a job to do. The company is relying on them more than ever. And you need their support to let the healing begin and reinvent yourselves as a team in light of this new and unexpected challenge.

■ ■ ■

The essence of Book 4—*Leadership Defense*—clearly focuses on treating employees with respect, holding them fully accountable for both their performance and conduct, and avoiding snares and land mines that workers or their attorneys sometimes set for well-intentioned but unsuspecting employers. The purpose of the book is not to make you paranoid; it is, instead, to raise your awareness of the challenges that may sometimes come your way when problematic performance, conduct, or absenteeism inhibits employees' abilities to contribute to your organization in a healthy way.

Our goal was to build muscle around leadership defense principles that all business leaders will likely need throughout their careers. With the shortcuts, tips, templates, and sample scripts you've been introduced to, you can feel more confident in your abilities to withstand challenges that may come your way. Above all, remember that treating employees with respect and dignity, focusing on your leadership, communication, and team-building skills, and sustaining a coaching culture based on selfless leadership will likely minimize your exposure to the at times challenging defense principles that you've studied in this book. When needed, however, you'll have educated yourself well, familiarized yourself with many of the traps potentially awaiting the unsuspecting manager, and prepared well to protect yourself and your organization from unwanted liability.

While not as sexy as some of the other topics in this book series on leadership offense, motivation, ethics, and culture, the employment defense topic is likely among the most significant and critical. I hope you now feel that much more prepared to deal with any performance or conduct challenges that may come your way. Thank you for allowing me to take this journey with you!

# ACKNOWLEDGMENTS

My heartfelt thanks to the finest legal minds in the business who helped with select portions of this manuscript as it made its way through the various stages of review and development: Jacqueline Cookerly Aguilera, partner, labor and employment, with Morgan, Lewis & Bockius, LLP, in Los Angeles, and Rich Falcone (no relation), shareholder and management litigation partner with Littler Mendelson, LLP, in Irvine, California. I can't thank you both enough for partnering with me on this book project and so many others. I'm so fortunate to call you friends, and I continue to benefit tremendously from your guidance and wisdom.

# INDEX

# ABOUT THE AUTHOR

**P**aul Falcone (www.PaulFalconeHR.com) is the chief human resources officer (CHRO) of the Motion Picture and Television Fund in Woodland Hills, California, where he's responsible for all aspects of HR leadership and strategy. He's the former CHRO of the Nickelodeon Animation Studios and head of international human resources for Paramount Pictures in Hollywood. Paul served as head of HR for the TV production unit of NBCUniversal, where he oversaw HR operations for NBC's late night and primetime programming lineup, including *The Tonight Show*, *Saturday Night Live*, and *The Office*. Paul is a renowned expert on effective interviewing and hiring, performance management, and leadership development, especially in terms of helping companies build higher-performing leadership teams. He also has extensive experience in healthcare/biotech and financial services across international, nonprofit, and union environments.

Paul is the author of a number of HarperCollins Leadership, AMACOM, and SHRM books, many of which have been ranked on Amazon as #1 bestsellers in the areas of human resources management, labor and employment law, business mentoring and coaching, communication in management, and business decision-making and problem-solving. Bestselling books like *101 Tough Conversations to Have with Employees*, *101 Sample Write-Ups for Documenting Employee Performance Problems*, and *96 Great*

*Interview Questions to Ask Before You Hire* have been translated into Chinese, Vietnamese, Korean, Indonesian, and Turkish.

Paul is a certified executive coach through the Marshall Goldsmith Stakeholder Centered Coaching program, a long-term contributor to SHRM.org and *HR Magazine*, and an adjunct faculty member in UCLA Extension's School of Business and Management, where he's taught courses on workplace ethics, recruitment and selection, legal aspects of human resources management, and international human resources. He is an accomplished keynote presenter, inhouse trainer, and webinar facilitator in the areas of talent management and effective leadership communication.